MARGATE CITY PUBLIC LIBRARY

8100 ATLANTIC AVENUE

MARGATE CITY, NJ 08402

(609) 822-4700

www.margatelibrary.org

1. Most items may be checked out for two weeks and renewed for the same period. Additional restrictions may apply to high-demand items.

2. A fine is charged for each day material is not returned according to the above rule. No material will be issued to any person incurring such a fine until it has been paid.

3. All damage to material beyond reasonable wear and all losses shall be paid for.

4. Each borrower is responsible for all items checked out on his/her library card and for all fines accruing on the same.

OCT   2018

The Coolest Monsters

the Coolest

Monsters

MEGAN BAXTER

Texas Review Press • Huntsville, Texas

Requests for permission to acknowledge material from this work should be sent to:
Permissions
Texas Review Press
Sam Houston State University
Huntsville, TX 77341-2146
texasreviewpress@shsu.edu

PREVIOUSLY PUBLISHED
"Lessons" was originally published in the *Carte Blanche Review*
"My Wrong Love Story" was originally published in the *3288 Review*
"The Coolest Monsters" was originally published in *Terrene*
"The Opal Thieves" was originally published in *Blue River Review*
"Letters to My Siblings in a Time of Apocalypse" is forth coming in *The Offbeat*
"The Wilderness" was originally published on the *Tin House Online Open Bar*
"The Lie" was originally published in the *Tishman Review*

Library of Congress Cataloging-in-Publication Data

Names: Baxter, Megan, 1985- author.
Title: The coolest monsters / Megan Baxter.
Description: First edition. | Huntsville : Texas Review Press, [2018] |
Identifiers: LCCN 2018008620 (print) | LCCN 2018017381 (ebook) |
    ISBN 9781680031737 (ebook) | ISBN 9781680031720 (pbk.)
Subjects: LCSH: Baxter, Megan, 1985- | Authors—United States—Biography. |
    Women authors—United States—Biography. | Women—Socialization—United
    States. | Coming of age—United States. | LCGFT: Essays.
Classification: LCC CT275.B427 (ebook) | LCC CT275.B427 A5 2018 (print) |
    DDC 920.72—dc23
LC record available at https://lccn.loc.gov/2018008620

Cover design by Nancy Parsons

For Daniel

CONTENTS

Lessons

I.

I AM TEN WHEN MOM shows me how to shave my legs. We are on vacation in a one-story beach house. My brothers and sisters are watching *The Swan Princess* on the TV/VHS player we brought from home. Mom takes me into the bathroom and shuts the door behind us. She shuts out the noise of the TV. I am wearing my bathing suit. She tells me that the first time she shaved her legs she did it with her father's straight razor. She cut up her legs. She went to a dance with her legs bleeding. No one showed her how; she had to make it up. So she tells me to sit on the edge of the tub. The memory of blood, on her father's razor, on the bathroom floor, on bundled pieces of toilet paper, on her dress. I sit on the edge. I put my feet up on the other side of the bath like she tells me. She shakes up a can of shaving cream and sprays it in my palm. I cover my leg thick with it. I wet the razor's lips under the water. Starting at my ankles, right where my socks end, I draw upwards in neat straight lines like I am painting a wall. Careful over the knees. Careful around the anklebones. Dipping the razor under the water. Stripping my legs back to skin. I wash my leg. I run the next one under the water and begin again. Thick foam, ankle to

I

knee. Moving slowly as I peel back, as I see each thick, rope vein, blue in my ankle, blue up my shinbone, then my legs are just legs. I wash my hands. I dry my legs with a beach towel that still smells like salt water. Mom takes the razor and puts it back in a little case. *Tomorrow,* she says, *we'll go to the drug store and get one. You've got to do it every day,* she says, *or the hairs will grow back darker and thicker.* My legs are shiny. My legs are smooth like the insides of shells. They want to be touched. Suddenly I have legs that want hands. Suddenly I have legs that are more than the sum of skin, muscle, and bone. They are polished shell, they are ocean rock.

2.

Walking up and down all morning, along the line of slick sand, I feel my legs, I feel my skin, I feel my hips, they thrust out like clock hands, setting the pace of my body. I look at people, at grown ups and kids and old men. I see them looking back. I have always felt invisible but now I see that I'm always seen. I don't know what to do with it but I know it, a shameful hot light. I divide the body into two categories. Things I like about myself and that I hate, things that make me turn up inside out and want to hide. But these two things are all mixed up. For the first time I feel the desire to rip myself up. I want to collapse in some parts and expand in others, like an explosion, breaking in and out, finding the weak points of the world, feeding on combustion, bright and violent and unavoidable. I make a list in my head, two columns against each other back to back, the things I hate and the things I love. And I go through my body dividing it between them. I give my legs to love; I give my arms to hate. I give my eyes to love; I give my breasts to hate. I give my hair to love, I give my stomach to hate so that I am uneven, I am unbalanced. Can I be a woman with only legs, hair and eyes? I walk the beach splitting along my own lines of constructions, wanting to pull out pieces of myself and leave them in the surf. Begging for eyes on the rest of me, like a TV screen static for attention.

3.

I don't let Mom hold my hand at the piercing studio. I hold my own hands in my lap. It's like a staple going into paper; the pain is quick and bright. A mirror is held up for me so I look at myself. At ten I have the eyes I will always have. My face is round, still a child's. My hair is straight and long. I have grown out the bangs that my mother used to cut across my forehead. There are shining green stones at the bottom of each of my ear lobes, on those soft, fuzzy plains. My ears are bright pink and they start to pulse. I have to wear the green stone in my ears for weeks until the holes heal. I am supposed to spin the backs in my ears to create scar tissue. I am supposed to soak the holes with rubbing alcohol every morning to keep them clean. My body makes demands. It has a schedule. Like school and summer. The woman hands me a card about caring for my ears. Afterwards Mom takes me shopping. We walk the main street of the beach town, looking at ourselves in the sheet glass windows. I see where we line up and where we don't. She wants to buy me my first pair of earrings, here, on vacation. She wants me to have them, always, as a keepsake, as the start of something. Mom points out things she thinks I'd like. I say no to all of them but I find, at the register, a neat list of stones by birth month. I was born as October faded to November. I am opal. Those pieces of molten light caught in ancient wood. I am that fire that always burns. I find a pair of Australian opal earrings, milky white shot through with purple, green and red, the colors leaping up at the slightest movement, at the slightest shot of light. They are cleanly mounted on silver. The opal is shimmering with its own veins of

3

iridescence so that even at midnight, or under thick sheets, or in the deepest part of the forest during a thunderstorm when day becomes night under the canopy, these stones will shine, these stones will catch something and hold that brightness to the edges of my face, like lucky stars.

4.

One night I make dinner. I have helped my Mom and I know all the steps. My siblings sit on the old couch in the rental house and watch *The Swan Princess* while Dad reads his book. Mom takes a shower. I put on the apron and tied it behind my back in a big bow. I fill a pot with water and bring it to a boil. I cut up garlic, *mincing* is what it's really called. I lay olive oil on the bottom of a saucepan and put the garlic in. I toss it around with a wooden spoon. I cut up cucumbers. I cut up carrots, scallions, and a tomato. I wash and dry lettuce. I tear it into smaller bits. I open up a package of ground beef and lay it on the garlic and I mash it up with the wooden spoon until it turns from pink to brown. I flip the salad with a fork. I put a box of noodles in the boiling water; spinning them around with a pasta fork. I lay the pasta fork and the wooden spoon carefully on a small plate on the stove. I pour a jar of sauce over the beef and then I stir the beef and the sauce together and then turn the heat down to simmer. I stir the noodles. I put a colander in the sink. I bring the salad bowl to the table. I take the bottles of ranch and Italian dressing and a can of Parmesan cheese out of the fridge. I put them all on the table. I count out six plates. I count out six spoons, six forks, and six knives. I lay the forks with the knives and the spoons on their own. I tear off six pieces of paper towel and put them under the knives. I pour the pasta into a strainer and wash it with water. With the pasta fork I pile pasta on each plate and scoop sauce over it. I put each plate between the settings. It is exactly like Mom would have made. *Cheers,* my Dad says, *to this lovely dinner Megan has prepared for us.* It tastes the same as if my Mom made it. I remembered all of the steps. I think of all of things I have learned. All of the dinners I can make. I want to know how to clean and cook, to drive, to pay the TV bill, to find the vacation home on the map. I imagine the table empty. I imagine the house empty. I imagine myself doing these things alone, cooking spaghetti and setting a table for one, in wonderful silence.

5.

In the heart of the night, in that time I have been told that the witches and black things come to the world, I wake up. In the vacation house with its wood panels. All the wood knots have eyes and they are watching me. I lie awake in the cot. My sister is deep in her sleep, wrapped in the covers but my ears are burning. I can feel the backs and the barbs and each piece of the earrings stapled through me. There is a pulse there like there is at my throat or my wrists. It gets hot and painful and then rushes downhill to nothing, and then it rises back up again. I am dizzy, spinning at the bottom of a pool in my sheets, wet with sweat. In my fever I feel like I am going to die. I look at its reality. I think about it. In the spring of that year I had an operation for my asthma. Dad told me that I could die, that I could slip past the reaches of the gas that was cupped over my lips and never return. He took me out in the field behind our house. He walked with me. We didn't look at each other. We looked at the brown field, the dead grasses of early spring. He told me that I was old enough to know that there was that risk. I said goodbye then. I collected all the things I loved and said goodbye. I lined up all of the dreams I had and said goodbye. But I didn't die. I was just fine. But I was ready. I look at that in the fever. Those lists, my dog, the woods, my graphic novels, my pocket knives, my siblings, my books, Jamie who I wanted badly to kiss, my friend Sawyer who I wanted badly to kiss, my dream home, my dream car, my dream of myself grown up, crushing cigarettes under the spike of my heels, climbing a ladder in my library, sitting in my garden as dusk. I don't want to wake my parents up. I ride the fever until the morning when my mother, cleaning my ear piercings with a cotton ball, touches one of the burning points and I pass out, fainting onto the tile floor, as the world slipped backwards into a hot, red point.

6.

In the movie, my brother and sisters watch all vacation as a princess is turned into a swan. She's cursed by a sorcerer for not agreeing to be his queen. Meanwhile a handsome prince is looking for her, traveling the dark woods and one night he sees her through the trees, turning from swan to princess on the moonlit sheet of the lake. We know his confession of love will break her spell but he is confused by the black magic and the swan princess dies. Enraged the prince kills the sorcerer and goes to the princess at the lake, he holds her lifeless body and confesses his love to her and she comes back to life, a woman with legs and breasts, skin and hair. They marry and live in a castle, looking down over the enchanted lake. My sisters watch this movie again and again. This story of a woman who has no choice in anything, in life, in death, in magic or black magic. As a swan she is white as snow. She is able to break the curse of gravity, to rise on the currents of air above everything, above the confines of the forest. Her prince catches just a glimmer of her woman form, at transformation on the water's surface, her flesh from feather, arms from wings, humbled, walking wet from the lake, her hair pressed down her chest, with only the contained memory of flight. Her curse is broken by love. It forms strong as a hurricane, moving across deserts and oceans, falling on distant continents, the coast itself existing as it as always existed, a blank line upon the map until it is transformed, until it is lifted by winds and rain. I learn to wait. I learn to be the coast expecting the storm. I pray for it to come to me.

A Princess Story

KATHERINE HAD AN ENGLISH PASSPORT and an accent, lightly, at the edge of some words. Together we pretended we were two princesses. Our parents died and we were adopted by different families. On the school bus we sat together. We clutched our backpacks to our bodies, as if they contained everything we owned. *I hope you like your family,* we would say. *I hope you like yours.* We waved goodbye to each other like it was a final farewell. At Katherine's house her father yelled at her mother until she cried. At my house sometimes my parents argued but only in their room with the door locked like their books recommended. Our houses were exactly the same, the same model built from the same blueprints, so it was almost like being home when I went over. All the angles were right but Katherine's family didn't have real maple syrup or carpet in their hallways. In our basement we had a big box that my Dad had brought home from the manufacturing company he worked for. It was full of dresses. Dresses my mother had made in the seventies. Princess dresses. Old Halloween costumes. Veils, fairy wings, mermaid wigs. My story was that I was being raised to be a knight, to avenge our parents' deaths. Katherine was being raised a lady; she wore the long dresses and wigs and taught

9

me how to hold a teacup and to sit with my hands in my lap and my legs together.

One day, in the rain, in a summer storm, we are sitting close to the old black and white TV my dad had in grad school, with dials and knobs. It's little, so we dragged our plastic chairs up to it. Every afternoon we watch *Dr. Quinn Medicine Woman* together. We were members of her fan club, we had tan bandanas and signed pictures of the cast. She was a princess in the West, a lady, she was always right even if no one believed her. The storm washed hard on the roof. My Mom yelled at us to close the windows, close the skylights, and latch the doors. But we didn't move because across the bottom of the screen text ran, linked, repeating like a paper garland. White on black. We followed it to the edge of the screen and back again. *Princess Diana has been killed in a car accident. Breaking news. More to come. Princess Diana has been killed in a car accident. Breaking news. More to come.* Doctor Quinn cut to the news station. Pictures held up on the screen while the text ran and ran. Her wedding gown filling a church, her little boys in their Easter clothes, her dresses, her jewels, her long gloves. The car, crumbled up like black construction paper in a dark tunnel lit by flashes, lit by cameras. Katherine was in tears. Her mother came to pick her up. The storms ran out into the nighttime.

The next day we felt the death of something big but the forces were beyond and past us. *The end.* Like the text at the end of a movie. One sentence. *The end.* Seat belts, tunnels, cars coming up hard against our imagination. The fantasy of it died so simply, *buckle up,* Dad would say, like how to lock the doors at night and not get into strangers' cars, or even look at strangers in their broad faces. It was the last time we spent together; after that, we stopped dressing up, playing pretend, sleeping over and making believe. That morning Katherine and I picked wild flowers, snapping their stems, holding them in our elbows like pageant girls.

In the woods, at a point in the stone wall where the ground rose and the sun broke through the trees, we laid the flowers down. We knelt at this alter. In the woods, by a stone wall built for sheep two hundred years ago when there were no forests, just rolling open pasture. We looked up into the sun, through the trees, through the leaves, the shade like stained glass shadows. Silently we said our own prayers. Our goodbyes, resting our chins on our chests. Tears ran down our faces. Rising, we left the wild flowers there to wilt and dry out on the stone. Their bodies gave a weight to things like a rock in the hands; the world became a story of breaking onto the hard plains of concrete, of glass, like birds, like falling bodies.

The Wilderness

WE HAD A BOOK. AND in the book, there were hundreds of pictures of the Civil War. The book was heavy and cool as a rock. When we were both eleven we held it between us, the left side would fall on his lap and the right on mine. We shared it slowly, gravely. Whenever our families got together, we opened the book.

In 1863, in a section of overgrown farmland that had been worked dead and then abandoned, two great armies met in tangled willows and thick pine. They bumped into each other, like blind men, before radios, or satellite, or even accurate maps. They killed each other with their hands, or shot into the wilderness, hoping to hit something they couldn't see. Wild pigs ate the dead and wounded in the night. From outside of the wilderness, in their camps in the cleared fields, the men heard screams all night.

A year of war passed. Moving in circles and turn-about the armies returned. The rotten ground stood again between them. This time, they turned up the bones of last year's dead. After the fighting and charging, sometime in the night, a fire started. First low, in the dense leaves and brush, then running up the trees like a flag up a mast. And again, sitting in their tents, with the wilderness like a black sea between them, the armies listened to the screams of the men they couldn't save as the fire moved through them and spread both ways outward. In one picture from the morning after the battle there are bones and ashes.

We loved the photograph of the burned bodies under the burnt trees. I think we knew that it was horrible. What we were doing was wrong, or it felt that way. The book sat openly on the shelves, but when we read it together, we hid. Or maybe it was because under the dead weight of the cover, half on my lap, half on his, our legs touched from thigh to calf and charged me like rubbing my feet on the carpet. I could feel him move against me as we flipped through picture after picture, pointing out the bones, the bones, the bodies.

We used to hide out by the northeast corner of his house, where it was always cold and in shadow. The woods came right up to the clapboard there, the blackberries and birch spilling over the stone wall like waves, rising back into the dark pines and up into the sugar bush. If I think of him at eleven, he slips away over the stonewall like one of the family's cats, and I can watch his white-blond hair fade away into the darkness like a white-tail running, into the wild places where it is easy to lose your way.

Sleep Away

THE FIRST WEEK AT CAMP I write "I don't love you anymore" and cut my ties to home. The lake is a flat black sheet. I remember the constellations and all of the dead people up there. There's the hunter with his club with the dog that won't leave his side. I learn to capsize and pull myself upright again. When it rains, my hands smell like the pages of my books. At night, I give away all my secrets. It feels good, this openness, close to friendship but divided by the broad plain of my honesty and my lack of fear. The moon sits huge on the lake, the water lapping away at the rocks and docks. I do sit-ups on the damp grass, one for each thing I did wrong, a hundred. I want to shape shift. I want to pull up my body at its weak points. I hate it. I hate it on the beach. I hate it in shorts. I hate it in the mess hall. I hate it at night in bed, in the showers through the crack in the curtain where I know the other girls can see. One at a time, crunching up the core of myself, of my hatred. In the moonlight. In the damp.

—

On Saturday nights we take a yellow school bus around the lake to one of the boys' camps. The girls in my cabin do my makeup, because I don't have any. They brush me blue and pink like

Sleeping Beauty's gown, sparkling glitter falling from my eyelids to my cheeks. I stuff toilet paper into my bra, forming a shape that is closer to what I want to press myself into, like molded wet clay. The boys stand in a circle in their dining hall. We walk in, and they surround us, reaching for the ones they want. The goal is not to be the last one chosen. The goal is not to be left alone. I am taken by the hand into the corner of the gym. We sway back and forth. I kiss his neck and his ears and his lips, and we rock like we are on a boat. His hardness is rubbing against my leg, his hand slipping down my back. My glitter on his collarbone is a memory to wake to. I sway off to a dream where I love myself, with my hands and tongue and become pink and beautiful at dawn.

—

The wind cuts the ocean gray with white waves and bites my cheeks, making them pink, making them hurt. Salt on the hairs on my arm. Salt on my upper lip like a moustache. Katy sits in the front. I steer and paddle behind her. I watch her back all day, her ponytail whipping, curling side to side. I love her a little bit. I want to know what her eyes look like in the night. She switches off from right to left. I follow her, opposite, stroking left to right. The canoes hug the coast, climbing up the little island chains of stone and pine. Wading on a tidal flat I cut my foot on a clamshell. Deep. The blood swells thick and rolls. The trip leader holds my foot and opens it to where there is bone, the colors pure as new paints. She wraps it but it stays wet. There is always the stinging tooth of salt. Cutting. Biting. I chew my lip all day in pain. I imagine worse things, I think about the book I brought on the camping trip, a book about the Civil War, about piles of legs and arms, about bone saws, about burning stumps shut. My foot isn't so bad. At night the sky is all dead stars and mysteries. Katy and I sit out on the smooth rocks and talk about futures. The salt in my eyelashes makes me cry.

A tree falls over the electric fence, grounding its shock. Frightened, the horses break out of their pasture and follow the camp roads in the night all the way down to the waterfront, to our cabin where the woman who cares for them sleeps. We hear the storm, snapping and pouring, but don't hear the horses as they surround us, in the night, in the rain. They circle the cabin, nibbling the grass, looking in the windows, swaying like tethered boats in the harbor. Dawn brightens their flanks, lights on their manes and on their broad noses. They wait in their silent circle to be brought back home. One of the girls screams when she sees them looking in like Peeping Toms. The woman who cares for them says *shh,* she says, *they can sense your fear.* She goes out and touches them, clicking at them with her tongue, lets them lick her palm. They come to her like they had been waiting all their lives. The horses follow her back up the hill, through the pines to their stables. Swishing their tails and swaying their heads.

—

The girls sit on the grass in a circle. Books are stacked in the center of our fairy ring, old library books, and hard covers. They smell of mold, of winters at the camp, of sunscreen and bug spray. We pass them around, cupping them, peering into their verses that are as distant as mountain ranges in the heat. Opening my journal I stare into the face of white, a snowfield, a hot sky at midday, shimmering. It is too perfect to ruin with my pen. I dip it down. I stop. I think of words like railroad tracks running through a salt flat. Connecting two things that before had been separated by impossible time and distance. One line then another. I carry the journal with me, near my heart, or stuffed in my pocket at my hip like a pistol.

Nebraska

IN THE NIGHT THERE WAS Rebecca. I never saw her during the day. We didn't sit together during meals or have any classes together. The summer camp filtered itself between the disciplines, writers with writers, dancers with dancers, musicians with musicians. She was in the visual art department, painting and sketching so her hands and arms and the edge of her face were always covered with something. She looked like she had been working in a deep mine. Her skin was very fair. The charcoal and bright chalks were like bad makeup, the blues and reds bruises and cuts. I remember only her skin and red hair. I couldn't draw her face or find her in a crowd. But I remember her, like a perfume.

At night the other girls went to sleep. I lay in bed. My whole body itched. When it rained the damp expanded my bones and everything hurt like my insides were too big for my skin. Late at night, Rebecca and I met in the bathroom. Sometimes I found her there. Sometimes I was there first sitting on the hard cement floor in the moonlight.

Her skin was like a snowy field. We leaned against the pine walls; legs out in front of us, whispering to each other like soldiers, whispering like little girls. When we said something of significance, silence sunk us and we looked up to the ceiling as if the room was filling with water. We sipped from the tiny plastic caps of Robitussin, which the camp store sold, two or four or ten bottles at a time. We used it to cure whatever ailed us. Sometimes we licked at it, candy red, our tongues circles the plastic measuring cup; sometimes we knocked it into our throats like a shot of whiskey. Once, the Christian girl who played violin poured out all our bottles in the sink. *You bitch,* we said, *we need that. We're sick!* We bought more at the camp store and kept them hidden from her in our one, private drawer.

Rebecca was from Nebraska. Sitting beside her I imagined her home from books I had read. I imagined the Great Plains, weather a person couldn't hide from, you had to let yourself be taken by the light or wind, snow or rain, like a boat on the ocean. I imagined rivers that had cut deep banks into the topsoil, and the quaking of the leaves on the trees that followed the waterway. Mostly I envisioned a limitless horizon, the edges of the sky just slipping, folding like silk at the farthest reach of vision. I had never been there. It was the Nebraska of Laura Ingalls Wilder and Willa Cather. Land of sunflowers, wolves and the last traces of magic. It was enough for me to imagine this. I never asked her otherwise. I held it to be true and I thought of her there, walking under that big sky. It made her strange and beautiful, like travel photographs and I felt that if I could know her I would know more of the world.

I don't remember what we talked about for those hours between dark and light, or the words that made us go silent as if we had spoken a great truth. I remember the feeling of the cement floor on the back of my outstretched legs and the wood on my back. How the humidity settled on the floor in the bathroom. I remember the night sounds in the great, beautiful blanks of our silence strung from word to word like black sheets on a cloths line. The water in the toilets and in the sink pipes. The other girls sleeping. Some nights they were very quiet, and then we felt as alone as we hoped we were. That isolation scared us just a little, as much as we liked it. Sometimes we shivered on the edge of things. Outside of the thin walls, the night walked through the cluster of cabins, rustling oak leaves like a kid in rain boots. Distant cars sped by on the state highway going between places we couldn't imagine.

Rebecca taught me how to shave my armpits, in the moonlight in the cabin's rusting mirror, drawing the razor like a brush over my body. I taught her to kiss like you are trying to kill someone with passion, which was the only way I knew then. We traced each other's limbs, like we were touching a pet. We braided each other's hair. We were happy to find the same pieces under our clothing, nothing like boys', just warm reflections of our own anatomy. Touching her was like touching myself.

The truths we shared didn't stay with me, but I remember seeing them there, like smoke rings above our lips. I remember the camp, all around us, breathing softly. I remember the loons, who called to each other with so much longing, and how their songs became a liquid that filled in the places at the edge of night. Our legs out before us, white and sticky, bruised on the knees. Our feet moving back and forth like wiper blades. Our hands touching on the cement floor. The silence of that. Just sitting, touching, feeling the blood pulsing through her, her skin so fair I could almost see her veins.

That fall, Rebecca and I both attended the boarding school that hosted the summer camp. The camp buildings spread out into the woods around the main campus so we walked the same paths as we had in the summer. She studied visual arts, and I studied creative writing, and we kept to ourselves, eating at separate tables in the dining hall. We had different schedules, organized around studio time and workshop hours. She lived in my hall. I saw her making popcorn in the microwave in the common room or watching her laundry spin in the dryer in the basement.

Once, during a fire drill, in the heart of winter, we touched again. It was bitterly cold and in the rush to get out of the building all the girls had wrapped themselves in their comforters and stuffed their feet in snow boots. We all stood at attention outside in the plaza between our dorm and the dining hall, listening to roll call. Everyone was very quiet, shivering and shuffling to stay warm. Above us, the northern lights shot through the sky, like serpents made of light, sweeping, creeping arches of green and yellow. In the strange fluid light I looked and saw Rebecca standing beside me. Our shoulders touched, blanket-to-blanket, and I remembered her translucent skin, the chalk, and ink like bruises on her body, how I imagined her eyes were different for having been raised under a huge sky.

I didn't think of Rebecca again until many years later. I had not forgotten her but I didn't draw her into mind, nothing reminded me of those humid, important nights, of our shared truths, the loose, rambling thoughts of cough syrup and exhaustion. When she came to me again I was on the road between places I didn't know. I drove to the southwest, through the badlands, the canyon lands, and the deserts, escaping what I left at home in the East. I ran away from myself all the way to the edge and then had to turn around. I started to feel like I was moving backward, not forward at all. Instead of growing up, I was becoming a girl again and I thought about the snow in Michigan, one winter it had snowed for forty-six days straight, and I remembered the smell of the heater in my dorm room. I spilled Diet Pepsi over it and lost handfuls of Goldfish crackers down its grates so it smelled, on the coldest nights, like sweet, artificial cheese. I remembered talking about art like it was a word that started with a capital letter with my suite mate in our joined bathroom then I remembered Rebecca. The cold cement floor of our cabin, how big everything had seemed and how close.

I was driving East through winter, a broad, flat winter in the West, and I followed a blizzard out of Colorado, over the Continental Divide and stayed with it, each day, state by state, the wind moving just as fast as my car. It was tight-knuckle, bitten-lip, tired-eyes driving. Whiteouts on the plains, black, white, every kind of ice, snow blowing, snow piling, the lights of wrecks and pull-overs blinking from the edges of the interstate. It was bad luck, maybe a curse.

In Nebraska, I stopped early for the night in a town called Gothenburg off Interstate 80. My eyes were tired from looking through snow all day and fuzzy around the edges. I checked into to a two-story hotel, the sort where the doors open to an outdoor hallway, the sort that always remind me of my dorm room in high school. The land there was flat enough that I could see the bright, mounted signs of the town from miles away. I got back in my car and pulled over to a Pizza Hut that I could see from the hotel. I walked from my car with my jacket zipped up over my mouth, my hands deep in my pockets, braced against the wind and the blowing snow.

At the edge of the parking lot, between the restaurant and the road, there was a little graveyard, surrounded by a wrought iron fence. Inside, three grave markers clustered together, also iron, but delicately rendered into twisted hearts and vines. The grass was tall enough to stick out of the snow and the blizzard's wind made it speak and rustle. There was a plaque and I read it, with my hands deep in my pockets, with the cold blowing straight from the side. Three children were buried there from the same Swedish pioneer family. Other children who were caught in a prairie fire may have been laid to rest there, unmarked, unnamed, tucked into the soft earth. The crosses were made of Swedish steel, crafted by a traveling blacksmith who moved from homestead to homestead, fixing pots, making horseshoes and nails.

Their small graveyard seemed miles away from anything. I looked around. The Pizza Hut sat ugly and red in the parking lot. The paved roads led straight through the place. Any barn or house or structure that might have been built by those pioneers was long gone. Burnt, blown away and picked over for pieces. Or maybe they had carried the bodies out here, away from their farm, and buried the children alone on that lonely edge of their world, in an effort to keep their sickness from the living or to keep their ghosts far enough away that they might never find their way back.

In the motel, on the edge of the interstate, with the slow traffic like water moving under ice, I thought about Rebecca. All blue and white and still half wild, but I loved her memory anyway. It made me wonder at all the secrets we shared, if they still could bear weight, or if everything we said was just an echo, what did we know then? I remembered her lips on my lips. Her hand on my hand. The night huge and dark around us. Our silence full of meaning. I thought about my imagination of her and of this place, how far away it had seemed, like another world, the flatness, the creeks lined with cottonwoods, the roads marked with sunflowers. The clouds rolling like waves, the grain in waves too, an ocean, a moving landscape, that ground eating up one, then another, then the last of those children, blond angels, the first of their generation to be born in this country. Their bodies marked by hard, Swedish steel. Everything I thought I knew I had imagined.

The Opal Thieves

OFF THE ROAD THROUGH THE desert I say *pull over, pull over.*
Dust from the tires. Dry spruce walking up the canyon walls,
over boulders bigger than cars. The river runs white through the
center, brown and clear at the edges. The riverbed flecked rainbow
rock colors, sharp pieces, soft pieces, and old stones. Jason lights
a cigarette. His long body leans on the hot car hood. He unfolds
in the light, plant like, governed by different principles of living,
fed on starlight, fed on rainwater and deeper streams than I knew.
He needs money but is no worker. His skills have no applications.
He wants to get rich stone hunting, gem mining, a California
dreamer. We are off to the mines, to the mountains, to the plains
of Nevada, with a cooler and a case of Mexican Cokes, sweet in
their glass. Sweating in the desert like shoulder blades, like necks.
In white I am my own vision of a teenage dream, on a desert
road, in a fast car. The white dress sweeps against my legs. My
feet in tight boots, the leather as blue as the sky. The Los Angeles
River runs down excited, late for its wedding to the great wide
ocean. Running down to its confinement, to the broad canals, the
cement, the slow, draining flatness of it all beneath the freeways,
through the bad parts of town, dragging out to the busy seaport,

a tortured river, stretched, made to run a bit further, a bit wider than it would. I take off my boots. I take off my T-shirt. *Come in,* I say. Jason shakes his curls, shakes his head, and taps his ash, *no.* I step in on the smooth bank. Shock cold. Lungs pulling inward like explosions in space, sucked in, self-devouring. The skirt like kelp, like a mermaid's lower pieces made animal under water. In the white, in the running, skipping part where the rocks have been rolled smooth and round as organs, I sink to my knees. *Current take me.* Pulling my skirt away, pulling my arms down, rushing over the ground we covered, on its own path. The cold in my throat, in my breasts, armpits, in the center of my body, running up through the space between my legs, taking a core reading of stillness, of clarity. Push up, muscles and flesh against water and gravity. Muscle and bone against the course of the ages. The skirt to my body like another skin. The cups of my bra filled, spilling out snowmelt, spilling out the rain that breaks at the top of the world. Baptized, I am priestess of myself, I am all the things known and unknown, which wakes me in the night, like distant coyotes, saying, *this isn't it. There is more.* Their calls give shape to the landscape, the deep places, the rock walls, the plains and thick forests, and in my throat, in my belly, I shrink and expand. The sun crisp on my shoulder like a golden backpack, the sun in my hair. All day, in the desert, in the car, the smell of this ceremony, sun, water, rock. I say these things until they mean something. I rock to it. I write it inside my mouth with the tip of my tongue, French kissing myself. Reading the roof of my mouth like the stars at the top of the world.

2.

The towns constructed during nuclear testing are just buildings now. Empty stores. Places for dust to settle. Parking lots to pull off into and smoke or eat a sandwich. Spaces on the map that still have a name. In ten years, when they print the atlas again this might just be highway, scrub land, a strip between mountains and mountains, a spot where the ability to break the world along its fundamental lines lit the sky like a hundred million thunderheads once upon a time. The sun has washed everything out like color can't exist here. Greens are gray. The road is black, shimmering above a ghost snake road in the sky. The distance wobbles in its reflection against the foothills. Snow on the Sierras, rising into a place where the sun has less power, where the ocean winds break themselves against the desert. There is one open gas station and we pull off to fill up. The American flag above it is a huge sheet, the red stripes are pink, the blue is gray, the white is transparent, through it shines a sky that is just particles, rising dust, chemicals. It beats against the pole. Keeping its own time, a clock running out of batteries. In the bathroom I look over the sink. The mirror looks back. I see myself there, a different self. I see age for the first time. It comes to me quickly, like a baseball falling out of the shadow of the sun and it hits me right in the face. I don't have time to catch it. I look again and again at this new thing at the corners of myself. It's in my teeth; I bear them like a mountain lion. Chipped from forks, from food, from biting at things, from my own nails and knuckles. Yellowed from tea, from wine, from nights of forgetting to brush before bed. The lines in them like ivory. The lines in them like geology. Lines of history, of joy, of cakes, bodies of men, bitterness, the tears spilling in through the corners of my lips. There are wrinkles running away from my eyes. They start small and then split like hairs outward toward the edges of it. My cheeks cast shadows, showing jaw and face bone, showing skull, giving it all away without X-ray or touch. Let the idea of age come to you like the news of a death, spoken very seriously, spoken softly and then, *what else to say?* It gives me depth. This bad light, this dirty bathroom. This look deeper into my face, at all the things that didn't leave me, the things that cut and drained, stretched, darkened the face of my soul. I walk back to the car with this inward picture of myself that I memorized. I pull it over my face. I let my teeth line up with the teeth in the mirror. A quarter of a life, the weight of that. Take the years and split them four ways and carry their weight over rib bones and jaws, standing upward against gravity. Struggle with the principles that control the breaking of light, that turn heat to snow, that turn light into fire.

3.

The hotel clerk in Reno, Nevada, says from across the lobby, *you must be Megan Baxter.* I am. The only guest in this building rising twenty stories into the sky. He has been waiting, like a gatekeeper, to take me somewhere, down a river, deep into a gorge. Our room is on the fourteenth floor, high above the strip, the lights, the parking lots. We drink tequila in plastic cups. Jason gets ice from the ice machine, fourteen floors down, and we bite it between our teeth, run it over our lips, drown the cubes in our drinks. There is a stain like blood on the chair, filling the bottom cushion and then more below the chair, spread out on the carpet like a starburst. It has been cleaned but the darkness is still there. On the TV all the stations come through with lines of static. If we turn up the volume only the noise of static increases, that itchy, loud, white noise, but the voices drown under it, too heavy to float to the top. We watch it anyway, looking through the static, listening through the static as if we could find something there, ciphered, hidden and taking it, divine the days. From the window I see the edges of the city run quickly into the black nothing of the desert night. We drink until we want to touch each other and then we knock and fight our way to love, pushing a lamp off a table, unplugging the clock, struggling to create the feeling we had one day, two years ago, on a beach in northern Michigan when our hands and lips first met in the darkness, in the snow, by the great dark lake, in the shadows of houselights that were like little promises that the world could get better. His poetry, his Pacific violence, his death swells and black sand beaches. My pine woods, my New England peace, my snow falling on the white steeples of a little town's church in the deep folds of the mountains, my old rivers and headstones green with lichen. We fight to find these things in the hot places of each other's body. Reach for it; pull it out like dentists, like surgeons. *There. There again.* Knowing the other is still what we imagined, our dream selves, still, embalmed, the rigid corpses of our fantasy. In the night the room's temperature rises. Falling from the ceiling, as if the building was on fire. I wake in a sweat that is capturing me. I wake with images of flames. We are too high to jump, the fear of smoke in the lungs, is the only thing that raises me from my sleep. But it is only heat, not fire. I drag myself to the window, a reflected ghost, breasts and stomach above the city. I turn up the AC; I stand before it, letting it cool my legs, my center, my core. The heat eats it up. I turn my back to it, I spin, waiting to breathe again without fire in my lungs, waiting for my skin pores to close, the wetness of my body spilling itself out down my arms, down my fingers, onto the carpet, leaving my cells, my stories there with the blood, with the stains that don't come out. Jason fights the heat in his sleep. I lay beside him. The sheets are wet. He struggles like there is a giant snake around him. I lay like a body lifting above a body, trying to rise out of myself, to float above myself, to become, just a projection, a spirit guide in a different atmosphere of cool, of a clarity like Freon, traveling through a better, truer night to the source of peace, to that place, under an ancient tree.

4.

A wet place in the desert where the water birds land and call day and night in the reeds. A pool between dry mountains, through a plain of dust devils, through a plain of wandering, dark cattle, towns like memories of towns, like sets from movies about the places like this. We camp outside the entrance of the mine. We learn to build our tent. We learn to set out our sleeping bags and light the camp stove. All of our tools rest in buckets. Our futures all gem and cut glittering stones. Light takes forever to leave the sky, draining it, painting it, sinking past us over the rim into the edge of the world, into the new places past and beyond us and slowly the moon rising, an abalone shell, and through the draining sky the stars, the bright ones first, the great planets and galaxies, the frozen maidens and brave hunters connecting place to place, light to light, moving through that huge darkness so vast that some of them come to us, the shadows of the dead. Our fire against this, throwing up sparks into it, fading, false stars. The frogs and toads beating at their primal throat drums. The desert sounds too, the dry shifting of rock and sand, the old, old mountains collapsing into themselves, the bottoms of the ancient oceans becoming the dust along dark highways, moving between points on the map that have names but no souls. Coyotes hunting, fast between the dry spruce, high in the canyons chasing a scent or the tail of red hunger down to its final point. Daylight comes early to this place, with no trees or tall edges to hold it back, dawn falls into our tent. We load the car with water, with tools, with our buckets of hammers and picks and screwdrivers. We cover our faces with sunscreen and put on baseball caps and sunglasses. Up into the hills, to a flat cliff under which a vein of opal runs, like an ancient river of rainbow, packed in with the ordinary rocks and skeletons. We paid for four feet of wall but we get to choose which feet. We walk until Jason feels good, as if something in there was talking to him, saying, *here, here, I am a rich and light and will roll into your hands like snowballs of gems.* Desert sun on our backs, the deep shadow of the wall shifts and keeps the time like a dial, spinning over us and out into the parking lot. There are others, picking, cutting, pulling out stones and holding them to the sun, looking for the fire in them. Some have dug deep holes, shoes out, bodies in rock they pass pieces back. Following the veins of the rock. Following the printed packet of instructions from the front office. Finding the soft spots. Cutting them out. Holding them up, spinning them, looking within them. Putting them in the rubble pile. Staying hydrated. Wearing sunscreen. Remembering to take breaks. The passion is all consuming, driven to the light in the rocks, the shimmering, preserved fire of ancient volcanoes, the real, future shape of Mercedes, the smell of cash in your hands, all that sweat, making everything, always better. It is easy to hope for things to be easy, to be lucky, to have the earth open up and lead you into her glittering chambers, follow her through the darkness, through the red and brown rocks that are only rocks and only ever will be, into that place of beauty, where destruction has become precious, where it has been preserved, like a memory of painful love.

5.

The stones are little and weak. They will break in the air. They will dry and lose their fire. They can only be held in water, these Nevada stones. We put each of them in a bowl of water in the cooler. Laid in like fish, shining rainbow trout. They move, shaking in a hundred colors, working the light into its gradients. We have been knocking out stones with hammers and screwdrivers. Looking for a line into money, into a big one, a hunk like a brick. Museum quality, a huge check. Following the flow of stone and time. I find a piece of preserved wood with an opal inside. The petrified fire of the sap, super-heated by volcano, turned into liquid rainbow. A stick of rock that when held up to the sun shines through like a bone hollowed and then filled with light, red, blue, blood colored, shifting between dawn and dusk, breathing like a living thing this opal. I put it in my pocket. A piece of ancient earth. A thing of death, of transformation. A phoenix rising. We dig and dig until our ticket runs outs. We put our tools into buckets and a lid onto the bowl of stones. We spend a night under the stars. *What is it worth?* This wet collection of gems, rolling together in the cooler? Jason dreams huge, casts those dreams up above the fire. We'll never have to work. We'll live on the road, moving between great houses, on the beach, in the mountains, on a hill above the desert. We'll fill our lives with books, books touched, signed by the pens of our heroes. We'll be able to open them and bring them into our living rooms and studies, like breath. We'll eat dinners out in Los Angeles and Santa Barbara, plates shifting before us, small, round pieces of tuna and oyster and raw, red cubes of beef. The riches will rub out our edges, our sharp points. We will fit together better, like perfect puzzle pieces. Our nights will never know loneliness. Our cheeks never tears. We will burn the world if we wish, or watch it burn itself, the wildfires coming down through the canyons on a fountain of smoke, eating through the homes of celebrities, coming down like a rabid animal, mad with thirst, to meet the great, dark sea.

6.

I start to suspect that they are worthless. It's a secret, a sense I have. The stones slosh and sink in their water, dirty and dull. We haul them like memory in the trunk of the car. Through mountains. Down their steep edges where the trees are like temple pillars, holding sky from earth, supporting the weight of the world on their ancient, vertical rivers. One trunk, a building, a wall, a divider between growth and our small, skeleton lives. The secret is a stone in the belly, worrying at things. Making a pearl of doubt there, irritating it all until the days are worn thin. The futility. The pretend. What is real and good: pancakes, dirt, sun on shoulders, fireplaces, old dogs, good boots, these things I wrap around myself in the front seat, I rest my head on them. At the motel Jason carries in the opals, stolen from the earth, their fire taken from them, white faces, bone knuckles. I can hear the water sway side to side. He opens the red cooler lid, hoping to see them transformed. Again and again he runs the numbers over in his head, lines up the accounts and sees again the cars, the homes, the money, the cash in hand. He sits on the bed and shows me which one is his favorite. Big and red but only when spun, held under certain light, a mystery of a gem, hiding its beauty, its fire, he rotates it, this dirty, sunburnt child of a man, this boy. Half in this world, running parallel on a different plane. To believe in him is to believe in the stones. To believe in him is to believe in the flash of the opal's fire, struck in water, like cooling coals. In the shower the water washes away dirt, desert, the sweat of the mine, sleeping bag, campfire smell. I stand under it a long time. Head up. Mouth open, water through and over me like I was a rock under a waterfall, like I was a thing shaped by waters. There is a knock on our door, a loud, sincere fist. Jason opens it to a police officer. Jason was trying to call out for pizza but dialed 911. *Everything is okay,* he says. I can hear the officer looking at the dust on him, at the bruises on his elbows, the desert on his cheeks, looking past him into the room to the cooler, open, like a treasure chest. He lets himself in. *Is there anyone with you? My girlfriend, in the shower.* He knocks on the door. I turn off the stream. I step out and get wrapped up and open the door just a sliver. *I'm fine,* I say. *I just need to come in, just to make sure. You never know,* he says. He opens the door all the way. Standing wrapped white, hair pressed, dripping onto the tile. My body tan, bones, curves, breasts, hips, toes, the ordinary lines of my face. He looks for my pain. *I'm fine,* I say. He nods, shuts the door. Goes out. Thanks us. In the light of the bathroom, in the long wall of mirrors, I look at myself. There it is. The weight, that stone in my stomach. No bruises, no cuts, no bullet wounds, just this drowning, this dark shadow of the things that were that I carry like a shoulder bag, heavy to my waist. I am not fine. I am not fine. I want to run into the hall and have him take me with him, to a cell, to a place with coffee in Styrofoam cups. To believe is no longer the thing. Even though we had promised to grow together like two old trees, twisting toward a shared vision of heaven. The fire, the light in the stone, the memory of more ancient pain burnt forever rainbow through the core of the standing world, shattering the sky in its reflection like broken mirrors, a hundred thousand different versions of the same simple body. The futures diverge. The past remains, a stiff shadow, a twig turned to stone, weighting me, saying, *from this spot you will not move.* My skirt pinned, pulling against the strength of all the old dreams, towards a place of high snows, the crack of thunder ringing through clear, deep valleys.

The Promise

IT WAS THE FIRST TIME I had lived with anyone who wasn't family. We weren't twenty yet; Jason had turned eighteen that fall. Our parents helped us move in, driving up with their cars packed. They filled our fridge with groceries and cried when they said goodbye. He was very far away from home, a continent removed. He had grown up on the coast of California, sitting on his father's porch off Pacific Coast Highway in Malibu, watching the sunset and now here he was, on the coast where the sun rises over the cold rocks of Maine.

We were high school sweethearts. We met at a boarding school halfway between our homes, in Michigan, on the dark banks of a lake. This was our first try at life in the world. We were going to college together. We did everything together. We planned on getting married when school was over. We wore rings, wedding bands that held that promise. We were both in awe of the other. We made each other out to be small gods. I watched him move around our home like he was sunlight; he was crystal, contained in human form. I watched him sleep like he was a marvelous creation that translated texts from ancient shipwrecks onto blank pages on Microsoft Word, rendering black their translucent lines.

Those first weeks we let each other live like kind ghosts. We learned each other's habits by standing at a distance and observing. We figured out our showering schedule, when and what we liked to eat. Jason's parents were artists; they were crazy California people, whose divorce, over a decade old, still raged like wildfire on the slopes of their existence, destroying Thanksgivings, birthdays and phone calls. My parents remained in a marriage that seemed so steady as to have lost the heart of everything, a soulless, respectful relationship. Jason had been a successful actor as a child. He had spent his money on Edward Curtis prints; nice sports coats that he wore over pajama pants and fancy dinners out. I worked all the summers that I could, as a baby sitter, on a local farm, saving, saving, for the day that I set up a little apartment. We knew these things wouldn't mix well but we resented these problems of everydayness, they felt beneath us, so we said nothing, we stepped over them like dirty laundry. We talked about Neruda, about Hemingway, about fonts and the shapes of books.

The house was a practice house. Our landlady and her ex-husband had built it so they could learn about construction. They made the little cottage and then lived in it while they worked on their real home right behind the place. It was maybe 200 feet away. The house was truly a miniature; it had all the details of a bigger home. It was pretty, and neat. It sat in the shade of big spruce trees and had a front porch, a winding staircase, and an upstairs with a queen-size bed under the eaves. We thought it was perfect; the only thing it lacked was ocean, and that was only a few minutes' drive away. We lived on an island off the coast. The ocean was closer than our college. We drove there every night. I packed picnics. We watched the breakers smash against the rocks. We walked the lonely, cold beaches of late summer. We told ourselves that we would wake early and watch a sunrise over the Atlantic, but we never did.

In the evenings, we were very alone. We went to dinner

sometimes in town, pizza, or Chinese. We rented DVDs and watched them on my laptop, resting the computer on the dining table, or on our knees in bed. We watched movies; we watched *CSI*. We watched until we were sleepy then we folded the laptop down. We were too young to buy booze. Once we drank up what his mother had left us, several bottles of Patrón, we were sober and restful nights slipped away from us. We were exhausted but found no cure. The nights were windy, and spruce trees brushed against the house. We were restless, tossing in bed, empty, only halfway to what we wanted.

One morning I woke before him and made breakfast, in a white tank top and panties, with my hair in a messy bun just like a girl in a movie. But I had stored our bag of flour near a box of Tide, so the pancakes tasted like detergent. We ate them anyway. Jason refused to go grocery shopping with me at Walmart or the island shop, it was too depressing he said. I made up lists just like Mother had taught me and filled up a cart with the ingredients for all of our meals that I had planned out on the fridge.

We both hated our college and talked about transferring. We looked at other colleges online. We did our school work, and read, and wrote. I had a desk downstairs facing the porch, and Jason worked upstairs, on the counter of a built-in bookcase. Neither of us amounted to anything. We were both too terrified of each other's talent to start or finish a poem or story. *Can I read it?* we would ask and then never write again out of the fear of it. I sat at my desk and looked out at the falling leaves, at the piles of red pine needles. I looked out at the first snow in October, and the early dusk of autumn. We had one trick-or-treater but no candy, so we gave him some granola bars. I felt terribly unprepared. I drove down to the grocery store and got more candy just in case. No one else came. The mice ate the candy. They walked our counters at night; they knocked spoons and knives into the sink.

One morning Jason found a mouse that had been hit by one of our traps. It was badly hurt but not dead. It walked in tight, clockwise circles, around and around in a fixed panic, dragging two limbs. Jason was nearly in tears; he couldn't look at it, he said, so I put it in a plastic grocery bag and took it out onto the porch. We discussed whether it was better to let it go and let nature take it or if it was better to kill it. I wanted to leave it for an owl or a fox and be done with it, Jason argued for a quick death. He was so sick with the idea of this thing being hurt in our house that I agreed with him. I got our heaviest saucepan and smashed it on the plastic bag on the porch until the little thing was still. Then I threw the bag in the trash outside. Jason was shaken all day. He couldn't look at me. We didn't go the beach. I made a spaghetti dinner with salad and garlic bread. I set our table, the windows all steamed up from the pasta water boiling, and we ate a solemn memorial dinner to the memory of the spinning mouse.

I got a job part time at the old general store in the heart of the island, just a few shifts a week, some of them very early, which I didn't mind, making coffee for lobster fishermen before they headed out. Some nights I would close, sell the last six-packs and cigarettes, count out the register, and lock the place up for the night. It had been a general store for nearly two hundred years. The owners used to live above the shop, but now the apartment was rented. There was a shallow stone basement where they kept back stock, I had to duck walking in and out of it. It was strung with cobwebs and always damp. The store sold a few groceries, lots of beer, wine, and cigarettes, Green Mountain Coffee, several newspapers, pizza, and sandwiches that we made up behind the counter.

There were three rushes a day, one in the morning for coffee, newspapers, breakfast sandwiches, and donuts. Then it was quiet for a few hours until noon when men came in for sodas and sandwiches. The afternoon was silent, long hours of cleaning and then staring out the window, reading the cover of the newspapers, doing some homework, restocking, then work would end, and men would come back for beer and cigarettes. Some of them would get a second sandwich. A few customers ate all three of their meals from the store. In the darkness the drunks would return for another round, a mother would forget milk for dinner; someone would come by for a pint of ice cream or a box of tampons. I made sandwiches and ran the register. I baked pizzas and cleaned the place. There was an icc cream window in September, so I filled cones and cups with soft serve when the bell rang for service, but that was closed down, like the rest of the town, as soon as the weather turned.

I liked the job. I loved the strange old building with its haunted sounds; its scary basement, the floorboards that bent and bowed like waves. I liked to think of all the people who had been there, customers and girls like me working behind the counter. I was a favorite; I got tips for my sandwiches and pizza. I did a lot of reading when it was slow. I got to eat a sandwich and drink a bottle of soda whenever I worked. One customer, a professor at the college, got a copy of the *New York Times* delivered daily. He caught me reading it one day and told me it was okay, so whenever I worked, if he hadn't picked it up, I looked through the paper.

I worked with a woman who had once been the local hot chick. She was aging and bitter and living with a logger. He had a mullet, and she would save pizza and sandwiches that were wrong orders for him. They would fight over the phone and then she would cry and call him back to apologize. The other girl who worked there liked anime and video games. She wore all black. She was dating a guy just like her, except he was fat where she was very skinny. They got married that winter at home and then went to the Chinese food place in town for the reception. The owner of the general store was an old hippy that had gone to college on the island and never left. He believed in small towns and good people and looked the other way when I stole wine and beer. I always put money in the register for it.

There was something happening, and I couldn't figure it out. It was like a slow tide. At first it started to snow. One night there was an ice storm. We lay in bed and listened to it beat against the roof like stones were being dumped on us, they rattled and scattered. The wind came in through the cracks at the edges where our landlords had only just been learning about construction. It got very cold in the house. We set up space heaters and bought another blanket but still in the mornings it was hard to walk downstairs. The floor was freezing to the touch. One day there was ice in the bathroom sink. I drew inward to save myself.

I sat at my desk and looked out. The driveway became a white rope, leading through the dark trees. In town, stores were boarded up, which I thought was just an expression until I saw the plywood nailed up on the storefronts. The beach was closed for the winter. We parked and walked to it anyway. We listened to the waves beat at the shore-ice. We watched a huge orange-pink moon rise over the islands on my twentieth birthday. It felt like it should mean something but it was as if I had lost my ability to speak a language, these signs kept coming, and while I was able to note their significance I was unable to interpret them, the mouse spinning clockwise, the way the ice fell on the roof that night, the big strangely colored moon. They just added up, like a bank against me, against us.

Weekends were slow at the general store. There was no pattern, no coffee, sandwiches, beer rushes, no tidal flow. One Sunday it was very quiet. I had the place to myself. I cleaned, I restocked the candy bars from the scary basement, and I pulled the cobwebs from my hair. I made myself a turkey sandwich and drank a Coke and watched the empty road between gray place and gray place, the cold island, and the cold mainland over the causeway. November was brutal, bitter, and silent. It snowed but the snow didn't stick. It got dark so early that you felt like a crazy person, thinking of going to bed and realizing it was only five-thirty.

I stood behind the counter in the old store and stared at the broad field of dead grass across the road, with the hollow, empty stare of small town girls, of girls who are prepared to cut off an arm or start a house fire they are so ready for something to happen. I knew how I looked, and I looked that way anyway. I looked like I had never left the island, that I would work there forever. I felt my face changing into that girl's face. Sometimes it felt good to know for certain how things were going to go, and sometimes I was so scared that I cried and couldn't explain why.

I was listening to NPR on the radio. We could listen to whatever we wanted, whatever we could find on the dial. The words just filled up the corners but didn't give meaning to the rest of the thing. They slipped off my mind and fell like ice on the floor, slippery and loud. At the top of the hour the program switched, and I remember being instantly struck like I had touched something electrical. The voice so close I could imagine the warmth of the breath. Springsteen's voice was like thunder rolling out of the clouds on some sandy back road, rattling the screen door on the porch. It was so close but so full of space, so empty and human. I was suddenly aware of all the space in the world and all the lonely people who were as lonely as me.

Two years before, I first heard Bruce Springsteen, sitting in my friend Alice's dorm room. Her father had died over Christmas break. During his final weeks, he had asked his hospice nurse to burn all of his music onto CDs for her. We listened to one after the other of those CDs silently, like it was some ceremony we were performing, sitting cross-legged on the floor, looking into the music for some sign, a message mixed up in the lines. We both liked Springsteen, we played it a few times before moving on. Alice burned me one of the albums, a greatest hits collection. The songs on that album were bright, shiny things, like cars parked in town on a Sunday, deliberate in their beauty, in their noise. I listened to them, but they didn't mean much to me.

Hearing Springsteen play *The Promise* on the radio in that little old store on the island in Maine on that cold, gray November day was finding a code to translate the signs that filled my life. It was so cold, the music so empty. He was so aware of the emptiness of the world. It was about trying and falling short but trying again. It was about third and fourth chances. After the last lines, the guitar and Springsteen's howl faded like the wind at the end of the road into the darkness. I listened for their last echoes in the dark space between songs.

I don't remember the rest of the day. I don't remember closing up or walking home in the night, with the headlights coming bright and fast at me. I don't remember what dinner I made for Jason, or what we watched on my laptop that night, or the night itself, our touching or not touching, or our uneasy sleep.

That winter I started to read into things. Letter by letter I learned the codes. I started rolling my cigarettes and driving out to the coast in the evenings. I listened to Springsteen on the CD player in the car. Some nights I drove just to hear that voice all around me, in me, through me, vibrating the seat, rattling the windows. I sat on a bench looking out over the harbor, at the lights on the cold water, at the few boats just coming in, with the music in my head, the lines rolling over each other, waves. Waves of music that was more like scripture than poetry. Lines got stuck in my head and became the reason I did things, went places; they defined the gentle rage that made me both angry and sad at the same time. They expressed my feeling of being trapped in something I built with my own, loving hands. I looked at roads differently, and I saw them not as leading to places but to things, the way to Bangor was also the path to freedom, to the wilderness, to a new bright thing called the future.

I shared the music with Jason as we shared all things but this one didn't stick for him, he never really understood it, he still preferred Bob Dylan or Neil Young. He listened with me, but it never became his. It was the one, the only thing, that was mine, just mine in our world of shared objects, common books, verses, shows, movies, friends, futures and pasts. Springsteen was mine. A god in tight pants and leather jackets and a fast car, with a voice like a werewolf and a guitar that was so simple you got lost in it. I moved into that world, onto the boardwalk, into the pine-swamps of Jersey, into the deserts of the Southwest. I became that girl in those songs, the one who knows there is a way out and goes look-ing for it in all the wrong places and then finally finds the golden ticket, or doesn't, and lives and dies small, aware of the greatness of things that will never be hers. Sometimes it crushed me like gravel. Sometimes it gave me strength. I drove and drove and sometimes drove off the island, but I always came back, like I was tethered. I opened the door and made the dinner I had planned. I did the laundry and swept up the floor and lay beside him in the night.

The spaces between us widened, like canyons in an earthquake, the earth split under us. I looked across at him as he moved away, sometimes it made him more beautiful, the distance, the light fall-ing across his face. Sometimes I wanted to turn my back, but we stayed together, believing in our story as we had written it, unwill-ing to work at anything other than art. Even that we let grow fat with dust, too afraid of each other's minds to attack it like it needed to be attacked, with a real naked passion that was afraid of no one.

I look back at looking at him. This painting of a boy that I created. He forgot to get his hair cut, so it hung in dirty curls, reddish blond. He spilled things on his clothing regularly, coffee, food, and ink. He had a dress code that adhered to no one else's standards, sports coats over soccer jerseys and pajama pants, flip-flops in the winter. I had to beg him to wear shoes when we went out. I watched him from a distance, making these details into myth as he breathed and slept and ate things from the fridge. We refused to acknowledge that we were people. We left each other when we were sick; we resented food, water, shelter, sleep, as burdens, weights that we were forced to bear. We didn't live with each other so much as we lived around each other, turning the other into a glass ornament filled with false light.

We stayed in that cabin through the winter. We stayed there in nights when the snow blew through the cracks in the ceiling, thin veils of snow. The day we moved it was so cold that my houseplants froze between the door and the car. When we stopped at Denny's for breakfast on the mainland they didn't have any tomato for my omelet, all of their vegetables had frozen in transit. Our books weighed us down; they were the material of our lives. Each one felt essential, like a manual to a fort we might build, tips for survival, ingredients for life. Boxes of poetry, novels, art books that we dragged with us from Maine to Vermont then across the country to Oregon. Paying their weight on freight trucks. Ruining the springs in my car.

Springsteen drove with us. Mostly he drove with me. The voice carried me across the corners of the country, into the canyons and valleys and suburban streets. He stayed with me at night, when the lights from the high school football field were left on and illuminated the low fog and the stray cats scattered on the roof of our apartment in Portland, Oregon. He stayed with me on mornings when I was setting out, for school, for class, or on those weekend days when I took the road out until I was deep in the country and thought maybe, of the story in which I didn't come back. About the girl who shows up in town with no past, a bright smile and lots of hope. She gets a job as a waitress in a breakfast joint. The road brings people and takes them away. It becomes a force like creation. It is always an option.

Take me back to that store in Maine, with the ghosts in the basement and the slanting floorboards that made you feel like you were walking on the deck of a ship, caught in the waves of a storm. In that place where I was becoming a character in a story that I didn't like, the girl with hollow eyes who sees herself among the ghosts in the basement. Springsteen's voice came to me like all the things I ever wanted to hear from above. His was a hand outstretched. His was a code that lay under the structure of road and road map, under my heart, head, and lifelines. You can read it from my palm. His was a voice like the voice of the wind, coming through the cracks in the wall, freezing me to the bone so that I walk, always, with those fractures. In Xrays those broken bits are bright as sunlight, shattered through my structure, rings of pain and escape, rings of hunger.

Heal the Sick

MY GRANDPARENTS CALLED THEIR COUNTRY house "The Rose of Sharon." *I am the rose of Sharon, the lily in the valley.* Fertilizers from a thousand-acre cornfield ran into their small pond where Nana kept a rowboat moored under weeping willows. Swamp monster green algae bloomed under the flat, Indiana sun. At night, one of my older cousins said, the pond glowed.

I flew out to visit them by myself. *You can sleep in the upstairs guest room.* Nana opened the windows and smoothed the pillows. *This bed is special.* She thought she knew what I thought was special. *Your great great grandmother died in this bed. She gave birth to all her children in it.* All night ghosts shaped like blood ran through me. The wood cold, dark, and slickly polished, dust on the windowsill, dust on the lampshade. Dust is human skin. Dust is space rocks and pet hair and lint, ground up bugs and tiny mites that eat us while we sleep. It made me wheeze.

My bathing suit and beach towel were dry. Elise and I rowed round and round like ducks. The cornfields hissed. Slime emeralds dripped from the oars. *Where's the bottom?* I poked. *Don't! It'll melt your skin!* The willows wept as their boughs were pulled down into the algae, arched like fishing polls caught to something monstrous. *Be fruitful, and multiply, and replenish the earth, and subdue it; and have dominion over the fish of the sea, and over the fowl of the air, and over every living thing that moveth upon the earth.*

When I was five my lungs filled, closed up, and I drowned, slowly. I had started to expect the taste of my pneumonia medicine like a bedtime dessert. Bubble gum and sticky and a bit of slippery something. But this was different. This was a shut down. If I gulped the air didn't stick. If I sucked it down and ballooned my chest up I was breathless again. Whatever was in the air refused me.

That night has been retold so many times by my parents looking for forgiveness. I don't remember any resentment. I lied enough to know that even the truth wasn't believed half the time. There were a lot of wolves and a lot of shepherds, crying out for help. When I remember the story I remember the boy dying but he doesn't. The sheep scatter like dreams. I drifted into my parents' bedroom and pulled at my dad's arm. *I can't breathe.* My chest ragged, the slurping-through-a-straw sound that I knew later meant I was under attack. They called the hospital, and a nurse suggested that I was probably lying, *she is of that age,* and to come in in the morning if I was still complaining. Dad tucked me in and read me a chapter of the *Wind in the Willows.* The sound of my bronchial tubes constricting, rattling like a night breeze in the reeds.

He turns off the light. Be quiet. I count. There is no time for a while.

Blue skin—the medical term is cyanosis—*can be due to a number of problems including asthma and other lung and breathing disorders. It often reflects insufficient blood in the extremities or low hemoglobin, the carrier of oxygen in red blood cells. Normally, arterial blood is bright red, thanks to the oxygen it contains. Skin color is a combination of your skin pigmentation plus the color of your blood. When oxygen levels decline, blood turns blue-red.*

I held my blue hands in my lap. My lips were blue and dry. I couldn't really see things for what they were. The tiles were a math problem. The tiles were like the tiles in my Sunday school room. There, I made a whale out of a balloon like the whale that swallowed Jonah. My blood was drawn out through needles and tubes. The lady doctor who I saw all the time for my lungs took Mom aside. I had to sit on the bed with the tubes in my arm and in my nose. *She only had enough oxygen in her blood to live for another forty-five minutes.* Mom's face white like I was already a ghost.

Though I walk through the shadow of the valley of death, I will fear no evil. I lead myself out and away. I am holding the staff, like Little Boe Peep, like the Boy who Cried Wolf, like David, a shepherd. I walk out of the hospital so close to death I am never again afraid of it.

Asthma sounds like a whisper.

Nana tells us a story. She holds one of my uncle's old teddy bears and speaks through him. His name is Alford the Mouse and his red bowtie is almost brown and his features are oily from many hands and his eyes are black little glass beads sewn into his head with red stitches. *Just beyond the pond, past the willows, on the far bank there lies an Indian cemetery. It is a sacred place. There aren't any headstones, just a pile of rocks in the clearing to mark that place as holy ground. At night, you can see them drifting through the trees. At night you can still hear them singing.* Elise and I row there in the morning. I tie the boat to a willow in a looping, endless figure eight. We find a pile of stones in a clearing. The oaks there were huge and ancient. The stones are mossy. We stand at a distance, afraid to disturb the spirits. A boy walks out of the woods with a Walmart *Thank You For Shopping* bag in one hand and a BB gun on his shoulder like a soldier. He shows us inside the bag, the bodies of three squirrels, wet and heavy, sleeping dead in the plastic, tails and heads and curved spines. We tell

Nana about the stones but not about the boy. *A ghost*, we whisper, *a hungry ghost.*

Dad has to dress us for church because Mom doesn't believe in God. We kick our legs on purpose as he tries to pull up our tights. We giggle as he ties our sashes in bows behind our backs. His hands are clumsy. Elise runs away from him down the hall and smack into the wall and falls over, passed out with her eyes open looking at the ceiling.

Mom has proof. She presses a bag of frozen peas to Elise's head. *How could I believe in God, John? I stopped when I was eighteen.* That week Dad reads to us from our illustrated Bible where every man has a beard and wears bright robes and all the women are smiling. I imagine God is like a king on a big throne, reaching down and moving people around like I move my dolls in their house. Mom says if God existed, he would have reached down and stopped the tree from falling on my grandfather, or pushed him away, or pointed him over to another tree that wasn't secretly rotten. If God existed he wouldn't have let that happen. Proof.

There's a whole pile of equipment keeping me alive. I have a nebulizer that turns my medicine into inhalable mist. Its huge gray box rattles and roars. I have to breathe from it three times a day. I have a clear plastic tube called a peakflometer. The game is to blow into it as hard as I can and see how high I can push the red line. If it hardly twitches, I need to take my rescue inhaler, fixed with a clumsy spacer so I get the right amount of mist. On the bathroom mirror Mom has taped pictures of colored fingernails ranging in a rainbow from normal to blue so I can tell when I'm suffocating slowly. I can't paint my nails; I have to be able to read them naked. I am not allowed to go to gym class. On cold days I stay in for recess. Cold and heat, grass and pollen, cats and dogs, all poison me. When I take my medicines Dad reads to me, over the roaring of the machine. I breathe in words.

*If we die, we want you to know that Uncle Rich will take care of
you guys.*

What about Nana and Pawpaw?

Nana and Pawpaw aren't able to.

Why not?

They don't believe in medicine.

They wouldn't give you your inhalers.

Dad was raised as a Christian Scientist. When he broke his leg,
people came in and prayed over him for a few days before his parents caved into his cries and brought him to the hospital. When I
got my baby shots, Dad got his too.

HOW I GOT ASTHMA

Inherited: On both sides my great grandmothers had weak lungs.
Nana sent me my great grandmother's wedding dress. Folded,
creamy silk. The woman was as tall as me, as slender in the waist
but her arms were tiny. I couldn't slip them up past my elbows.
She never worked a day in her life, never gardened, or picked up
her children (there were nannies and staff for that), never carried
baskets of laundry to the line or stacked wood. She sat sickly,
indoors, trying to cure herself by:

Rubbing mustard oil on the chest

Inhaling steam

Inhaling steam seasoned with onions

Drinking fenugreek of ginger and honey

Smoking cigarettes of belladonna, strammonium, atropine

Sipping strong coffee

Sitting in warm baths

Inhaling ether

These are the things I'm afraid of:

Running
Sports
Temperature changes
The vacuum cleaner
The duster
Winter air
The oil that gets on my hands after I pet Elise's cat
Being sick forever.

Oh, but when Peter pushed Clara's wheelchair into the alpine valley, and that city girl takes her first free steps in the meadow, holding Heidi's hand, I cry, I cry, I cry.

We acknowledge Jesus' atonement as the evidence of divine, efficacious Love, unfolding man's unity with God through Christ Jesus the Way-shower; and we acknowledge that man is saved through Christ, through Truth, Life, and Love as demonstrated by the Galilean Prophet in healing the sick and overcoming sin and death.

—the fourth tenet of Christian Science

HOW I GOT ASTHMA

Environmental: From the great power plants along Lake Erie and the funnels of factories in the Rust Belt, burning up through the chimneys of the production lines on the east coast of Lake Michigan, sulfur dioxide (SO_2) and carbon monoxide (CO) churn in the clouds with oxygen and water, creating a chemical stew of acid compounds. The strong currents of the jet stream pull this poison away from the air above where it's formed and drop it a few hundred miles to the east, over the forests and towns of New England. Melting the faces off stone statues. Turning forests dead red on the summits where the toxicity is the worse. Drive through the White Mountains and see the pines reduced to skeletons. Stare into the fishless lakes. And when it rains, and when it snows, the SO_2 and CO particles fall in my lungs too. Dad blames himself for moving us here, to this gentle town in the valley between New Hampshire and Vermont where the Connecticut flows past our little college town, *the sort of place to raise a family.* We live with our doors unlocked but we aren't safe.

The Prayer of faith shall save the sick. . . . The beneficial effect of such prayer for the sick is on the human mind, making it act more powerfully on the body through blind faith in God. . . . It is neither Science nor Truth which acts through blind belief, nor is the human understanding of the divine healing Principle as manifestation in Jesus, whose humble prayers were deep and con-scientious protests of Truth—of man's likeness to God and unity with Truth and Love.

—12.1 Science and Health

Would they let me die?

I understand prayer. I understand the body's power over the mind. My doctors are worried that I take so much medicine that one day it might not work as well. They recommend meditation and acupuncture. They recommend that I learn to treat myself. I hate it at first. I'm playing badminton on the front lawn in the summer when I feel my throat starting to strangle itself so I run up the porch for my inhaler. Mom stops me. She sits with me on the steps, looking into the field. She holds me between her legs, with my back to her chest so I can feel her breathe. With me. In and out. Deep, steady breaths. She takes the metronome from the piano and sets it up by my bed, the needle dips and rises, one breath then another until I have gone from *staccato* to *legato.* She's been practicing the piccolo part from *Peter and the Wolf* in her music room, screaming, warning, *a wolf!* Sometimes she messes up and doesn't make a sound; instead, I can hear her lips touching the metal mouthpiece, her breath blowing through the holes. I learn that sometimes I want my medication because I'm afraid.

I can give myself an attack just worrying about it. Mom gets me a little purse so I can carry my inhaler with me everywhere and never worry. But sometimes I forget it, I leave it in the car, or up in my room while I am out in the yard and the fear comes to me again and I remember drowning, I remember air with nothing in it, and in fear I start to slip, mind over body.

When Nana and Pawpaw come to visit it is like a pilgrimage. This is sacred ground. Just north of our house, along the rocky side of a mountain, in a tiny town named Rumney, New Hampshire, Mary Baker Eddy, the woman who dreamed up, wrote down, and sold Christian Science to the nineteenth century world, lived a few sad years with her second husband. The house looks like all the other houses in town. An old, white saltbox, surrounded by big, green hostas and stone. Around the corner there is a farmhouse, falling in on itself, with a hand painted sign over the front porch, which reads *Whirled Peas*.

It was very lonely and dark there 150 years ago. People died all the time from things no one could see or understand. The wilderness was a character too, a devil. It killed people, and stretched up the flanks of granite-toothed mountains and into the stomachs of cold, tannic lakes. The soil was fertile in the valleys but all that good land was already taken, fought for and settled. Only the stony places reminded, where the topsoil was just a thin skin over granite bones. Where white pine and blackberry thrived, where sheep could nibble out a living, but cows grew thin and gave creamless milk. Mary Baker was born the sixth child of a religious man, who forced her to pray through the stone cold days of those years. She was the village beauty, with strange dark eyes that look through and out the camera lens. Thin and often sick, she complained of a painful eating disorder and fell into fits and seizures. Mary would seek treatment throughout her life for a variety of conditions. Critics said she sipped morphine. Others insisted that it was instead powerful prayer that warmed her bones.

In her later years she wore diamonds and fine black silk dresses. She was attended like a prophet. Just prior to her death, four psychiatrists deemed her *an excellent and capable old lady,* without any form of insanity.

From an ad Mary ran in the spiritualist magazine, *Banner of Light*: *Any person desiring to learn how to heal the sick can receive of the undersigned instruction that will enable them to commence healing on the principle of science with a success far beyond any of the present modes. No medicine, electricity, physiology or hygiene required for unparalleled success in the most difficult cases. No pay is required unless the skill is obtained.*

I'm sitting on the floor in Elise's bedroom. We're placing Perler beads on their sticky plastic boards. Once the beads are set we'll carefully carry them downstairs and have Mom run her iron over them, fusing the singular beads into bands of solid color. It's magic, this transformation, like ice to water to steam. I'm taking my medication through the nebulizer and reaching low with the tube bitten between my teeth, I inhale a bead through the mouthpiece. I don't feel it going down my airway or lodging in my lung but I start to cough and cough and the coughing goes on for months until the doctors recommend threading a scope down into me to take a look and see if they can find that little bead. Grown over with slimy lung mush. All pink and wet and angry.

First they take me to a therapist.

Am I coughing to get attention?

Is the bead real or did I imagine it?

Could I stop if I wanted to?

Is my subconscious making me cough, as a way to show the world that my mind is sick?

Has anyone touched me in a bad way?

Are you happy at home?

I try every morning to stop. I prescribe my own medicines. I have a little vile of baby M&Ms from Halloween and I knock one out in my palm each day like a pill. I swallow it without chewing. I feel better for taking it but I still cough. I make potions, like the powerful good witches in my books. I melt vegetables into syrup, distill the sap of houseplants into tonics, I drink pickle juice and slip a clove of raw garlic in my lip like a huge wad of bubble gum. I know the outdoors is good for me. The secret garden healed Colin, and he realized his legs were just weak, not broken. Maybe my lungs are just weak; I fill them with sunlight.

Later I read that Frances Hodgson Burnett fashioned *The Secret Garden* into a metaphor for healing, inspired by Mary Baker Eddy's Christian Science theories.

Is anyone pregnant? Pawpaw is asking as he sprays insecticides over the grass at our feet. The thick green algae pond breeds vigorous insects, super bugs with no reaction to DEET, strong enough to drill through our jeans. The whole family is gathered for a wedding reception on the lawn of Rose of Sharon. I tuck my feet up underneath me on the rented metal chair as he sweeps by with the hose and bottle. He looks like the old man version of my Dad and my three uncles. Not wiser or more respectable. *You would let me die,* I think as he kills the bugs.

April. Ten years old. Fourth grade. Tomorrow I have surgery. A tiny video camera is going to travel through my airways like The Magic School Bus, documenting each turn and bronchial tube, hunting for the cause of my chronic cough. Dad wants me to know the truth. The truth, he believes, is more important than believing. He told me Santa was made up when I was three to save me from the burden of believing a lie. *Things are either black or white,* he says. Good or Bad. We're walking together in the field, in the field where I play fairies and Indians and princesses and pirates, where I tent out in the summer, where I dream *The Secret*

Garden dreams, where I walk the alpine meadows with Heidi, full of daisy flowers and high grass, but the field in April is gray and the snow has pressed the grass low like dirty hair. The trees are bare. The soil is mud. Distantly I can hear the brook raging with snow melt. Our mud boots slurp through the slime. The sun is warm but the air is still chilly. I bury my hands in my pockets. *I want you to know that there is a chance, a very, very small chance that you'll die during the surgery tomorrow.*

One out of 100,000. But I don't know that. Very, very small seems big to me. One out of 100 maybe. One out of fifty. What do those numbers mean anyway if the one is me?

Dad remembers playing with an Ouija board with his four siblings. Nana was touching the planchette. I imagine her with the same, tightly permed curls, the same light blue eyes and vivid pink lipstick. They were in a darkened room, with a few candles flickering. Nana's hands swept back and forth over the letters too quickly to string them together, but then the phone rang, and she rose to answer it. He could hear her taking the phone into the private alcove near the stairs. Dad sat around the board, waiting until she settled herself back between her children. *That was John F. Kennedy. He wants everyone to know that he's in heaven now.*

For twelve months Mary Baker Eddy heard a voice calling to her. It would call three times, in ascending scale.

Mary.

Mary!

MARY!

Finally she answered in the words of Samuel, *Speak, Lord; for Thy servant heareth.* Never again did it call to her.

Magnetizer. Mesmerism. Animal Magnetism. Hypnotism. The Laying on of Hands. Angel Visits. Prayer in absentia. Mental malpractice. Malicious malpractice. Mental influence.

I wrote goodbyes to everything I loved.

Looking up into surgical lights, I counted backwards. The gas tasted like bubble gum. I'd requested that flavor from the anesthesiologist who I regarded, solemnly, as a potential executioner. When I woke up my throat is on fire. Torn out from the lungs up. I could hardly swallow. I let myself drool like a crazy person. But the cough is gone. They didn't find a bead, just lungs, violently pink, agitated and worn raw. Then, for two weeks I'm left in the children's hospital under supervision to see if I'm just crazy, to see if I'm a liar.

It was early spring. Easter. There were eggs hung in the trees below. I watched my parents leave me every night. I turned my lips green with popsicle sucking, lime's tartness like a bitter root down my throat. Standing at the window one night I thought for the first time that if I jumped I could kill myself. *My body in the trees with the eggs or broken on the pavement.* I've thought for many years about this brush against that dark sleeve, it felt like velvet on my cheek, it was hard in my mouth and as cold as pearls. Looking at myself looking at myself in frigid glass, while the nurses clicked around the halls, and other kids cried or wailed or bit their tongues in greater pain, I realized I wasn't in a story. I could jump. Or I could crawl back in bed, wrap around my pillow and open a book.

Inheritance

JASON'S FAMILY AND I PLANNED on going to Pueblo to watch the
dances, but police officers stopped us at the bridge over the Rio
Grand. In the night, a gang had kidnapped a rival, driven him
to the middle of the high bridge over that canyon and thrown
him down, onto the rocks. Helicopters hovered above the scene.
There was a crew at the bottom, collecting his body. We pulled
off the road. Jason's grandmother was enraged. She argued with
the cops. She told them that she had paid taxes to the town and
the state for fifty years and that she had the right to drive over
the bridge no matter what. She had the right to see what there
was to be seen. The officers were busy with cars, and eventually,
they let us all slip past them and walk out onto the bridge. She
looked back over her shoulder at the men in uniform, shaking her
head at the state of the world. We stopped in the middle of the
span, where the gorge fell empty below into the thin green river.
The distance was further than understanding. The water and the
rocks lay below in an imagined place. There was no bottom to
the world, just this flattened attempt at seeing something so far
away. Men in bright vests crawled over the rocks like tiny spiders.
A helicopter pushed the waters of the Rio Grande back, creating
a white circle beneath it.

Jason's grandmother dipped her head over the railing, hoping to see guts and blood, a body broken up into many pieces. She wanted to see the whole ugly scene, this murder that had taken place in the night, in her town, just a few miles from her home. The men seemed to move very slowly at the bottom of the canyon, like the distance slowed time. I looked until I was dizzy, until my stomach came up high in my throat. Jason's grandmother believed that we all needed to see what was destroying the world. *Drugs,* she said, *Mexicans.* She told us about the heads that were found in the desert. *Decapitated.* The bodies buried separately, miles away. She told us about paths through that wasteland filled with the dead, the bodies of women, children, dead from thirst, from exposure. *As long as they only kill each other,* she said. As long as the man they threw over the bridge was like them, a smuggler, and a dealer. She wondered how much of the body was left down there, if the skin was still readable, if they could tell what gang he belonged to from his tattoos or if the fall had shredded him a hundred ways and they would have to piece it all together on a table later.

We went to the Pueblo dances and bought fry bread and earrings made from shells. Jason's grandmother told us she remembered when all the Indians were skinny and beautiful. She was friends with many artists who had paid them to model, these lean, dark people. They had become famous painting Indians and the plains, the mountains, the adobes in town. Together they met at Doc Martin's at the Inn and drank martinis or whiskey; the ice in their glasses applauded them, these children of pioneers. Jason's grandmother's eyes were blue and light, clouds past through them like the swirls in glass marbles.

When she talked she left the world briefly, only her voice remained, holding her to this place. She felt that everything that was beautiful was behind her. Her husband's sports car sat in the garage like a caged jaguar, covered in oilcloth. She didn't need to drive it; she would just lift up the cloth and brush its cold metal body and feel the wind in her hair again. She looked like a starving person. Thin, skin stretched between bones. I wondered how long it had been since she took pleasure from the world as it was.

Driving back across the plains there was heavy silence in the car. We watched the sides of the road as we passed, the spaces spread between fence post to fence post. I noticed that all of the horses were standing in pairs, nose to tail, flank to flank. Dozens of them. There was something threatening about it. Like the bodies of families frozen in the ash of Pompeii. The horses were waiting for something that we didn't know was coming. A strange undercurrent ran through the world. It was a thing below the thing I understood. Jason noticed it too. Nose to tail they rested, gently, standing north to south like compass hands. Every horse, in every pasture, standing like that at sunset, arranged just so.

Every item in Jason's grandmother's house was labeled in anticipation of her death. She had collected artifacts for as long as she had lived in Taos and had become a personal museum. There were pots made by hands a thousand years ago out of mountain clay organized on the shelves in the bathroom. There was an eagle feather headdress on top of the refrigerator. Rifles filled one wall in the living room, stacking up like rungs on a ladder. Every surface was covered with painted hides, daggers, beaded bags and dresses, dolls, figures, and sacred shields. It was haunting to be surrounded by that history, the spirits were very ancient and very present in them, the pots with fingerprints dried in the clay, the hides tanned with urine and sweat.

She didn't want her three children fighting over her belongings so, methodically, one evening at a time she had tagged every item. Some of them were tied on; others were marked with yard sale stickers. When all her children were present, for Christmas and birthdays, she would auction off artifacts, collecting the ones she felt would be argued over and offering them to her two sons and her daughter so that everything was divided evenly. The dresses and hides. The pots. The jewelry. The weapons, headdresses, paintings, and sculptures. These little tags hung from each piece in the house, prophecies of death.

It was a house I was afraid to move in, to break something, or drop a stain onto a rug. The pots on the shelves in the guest room seemed to watch me all night. They were so practical, these objects crafted to carry water, or hold grain and grind medicine. Some of them were painted, but mostly they were plain, simple things, like our Tupperware and mixing bowls. Only their age made them extraordinary, these everyday lives captured, collected, given a name tag and always, even if it was unstated, a price.

Later in the evening we ate dinner out on the patio, as the warm night settled between the strings of lights in the trees and candles on the table. Jason's grandmother waved her cigarette like a conductor and told us about her family's gold mine. It lay high in the mountains, on a ridge above the Taos ski way. It was just an open shaft like an eye in the rock. As a young woman, she had hiked up there with her first husband, short of breath, bright in the face, her hair pulled back in a bandana. They had eaten sandwiches and looked down at the apron of the plains, leading up to the brink of the Rio Grande.

She drew us a map on a paper napkin as she sipped vodka out of a tall glass like it was water. She hung empty blue vodka bottles in the trees of her backyard, to capture bad spirits, she said. They shook gently in the night, like delicate chimes, breaking the light a hundred ways blue over the patio and across the face of her adobe house. Her map started where the trail turned away, following a valley up to another ridge line. As she drew, she described it, fifty years ago, like she was walking it as she spoke. She noted right and left turns at fallen trees, huge boulders, then uphill for twenty minutes, and after that the tree line would fall away, and the bald stone top of the world would stretch out. From there she told us to follow the lines cut into the rock, zigzagging deliberately to keep away thieves, skipping from stone to stone, up to the mouth of the mine.

The next day we carried her napkin map with us, as well as another of the trail system. The morning was hot and bright on the plains; light flattened the distance so that the mountains seemed to rise right at the edge of town. We parked in the shade of spruce and pine at the base of the ski way, closed for the summer. All the homes around it were all dark, and their driveways full of brush. Jason had more hope than anyone I had ever met. He could talk things into being. He could create gold from words, an alchemist, a believer. We shouldered our backpacks and walked up the trail. It was quiet on the mountain, silent along the broad fields, along the dry streambeds, in the new growth and old stone shacks. The weight of altitude pressed and our breathing became deliberate. At a sweep of a turn, Jason took his grandmother's map from his pocket, and we followed her words higher into the hills.

There, trees grew smaller. We heard nothing that would tell us which century we were in. The sun passed between clouds and then the clouds became a solid, bruised mass. Thunder rolled to the North, through the forested valleys. At tree line, we could see the storm, bright and fierce, coming up through the ski way like a wave in the sky. Jason wanted to push on, we would take shelter in the mine, he said, but then we could feel the electricity, and then we could feel the air crackle and the little hairs on our arms and ears rising up to align with the storm.

We looked at each other and ran. Our eyes were shining and white with fear. The thunder was right above us as we fell back into the cover of the trees. The light was now the light of twilight. We slid and skipped and rushed down the path we had just struggled up. Sweat rose on our cheeks, in our armpits, in the soft curve of our lower backs. Our hearts were beating at a rabbit's pace. The storm was behind us, on our heels, like a wild black dog, and the wind was pushing the trees around; the sky was breaking up, cutting at itself, shattering along its banks and towers. Thunder rang off each tree, each rock, so every sound had its own, louder echo. We made it to the car as the heavy rain started. We slammed the doors and sat in its safety. Blood was pounding in our ears. Sweat and rain soaked in our hair, flattening it to our skulls. Thunder was rolling in the mouth of the valley. Lightening white and purple, blue and golden, crossing and moving through the atmosphere as if there were no rules anymore, no up and down.

There were certain things we didn't speak about. We let them teeter on the brink of our separation, on either side of the canyon that was widening between us. We had survived by rationing the memory of good times; we had divided that joy until there was nothing left, just crumbs in our hands. We didn't talk about money, jobs, or when airplanes were coming or going. We didn't talk about homework, deadlines, or grades. We tried, for many years, to remain high above the world, in the thin air, like birds. We spoke of poetry, myth, and futures crafted from words, luck, and grace. We didn't speak about death. Or fear.

We sat in the car, the rain a river over the windshield, and didn't say a word about how close we had been to a bright, electric end on the mountain. We let the idea of death rest with us, in between our bodies on the center console in that place where I kept my purse and my iPod. We didn't name it or look at it; we just let it darken the edges of the day. Like the smell of wood smoke in my hair. Like the taste of stone.

Driving back we had to stop, we had to pull over, again and again. The rain fell harder than the windshield wipers could clear. It fell solid, like a waterfall. The day was like night until the clouds moved past us, over the plains, and we could look at the flank of the storm, stretching from the earth to the top of the sky.

That night we slept with empty pockets. We slept without. The bed in the guesthouse was two mattresses pulled together. There was a gap between them. The gap pulled us apart, pushed us further from each other. So we slept without touching, each on our side. With the gap in the mattress and the pots on the walls, we dreamt our separate dreams, his I will never know.

Mystical Child

IT'S THE LAST NIGHT OF the Newport Folk Festival in 1965. Bob Dylan has faithfully covered his best songs for a devoted crowd over the past few days, but when he steps up to the mic wearing a leather jacket and dark bell-bottoms, he's backed by The Paul Butterfield Blues Band and he's slung a 1964 solid body Fender Stratocaster across his chest. He holds it awkwardly but with great commitment, like it's more of a statement than an instrument. Dylan's got his signature harmonica strapped above it and when he sings he leans in close to the mic so he can be heard over the band. It's not him wailing on blues guitar but Mike Bloomsfield, off in the darkness of the stage, and when Bloomsfield opens up on the strings Dylan pulls back and watches him. There isn't enough lighting to cover them both, so instead the focus is on Dylan, though Dylan is playing, essentially, backup guitar to Bloomsfield. He performs "Maggie's Farm," "Like a Rolling Stone," "and "Phantom Engineer" (an early version of "It Takes a Lot to Laugh, It Takes A Train to Cry") and then walks off into darkness. The noise from the crowd takes shape. First it's just noise and then it forms into boos. The crowd is booing at Dylan. And while some will say they are booing about the short set, or that they are booing at the poor sound quality, most agree that they are booing because electric means betrayal, means departure, means their leader is leaving them via rebirth. The whole crowd takes up the booing until Dylan reappears and plays two acoustic songs, "Mr. Tambourine Man" and "It's All Over Now, Baby Blue." He leaves stage again to applause and cries for more. Dylan won't return to the Festival for another thirty-seven years, and when he does he appears wearing a fake beard and a wig drifting through the audience, reborn again as the crowd that cried Judas!

ISIS

First born to the god of the earth and the goddess of the sky, she is a beautiful woman with a throne on her head and widespread wings. She contains her magic in knots and wears a braid around her neck. Sometimes she holds a lotus or a sycamore tree, or a pharaoh, nursing at her breast, or she is the sycamore tree with a breast that the pharaoh drinks from. Or she is a kite, hunting the banks of the river high in the updrafts. On the prow of the boat of the dead she waits with her wings outstretched. When her husband was murdered, she went questing for his beloved body. She became a huntress, gathering the pieces of her husband from the corners of the earth. She collected thirteen parts but, alas, the fishes of the river had eaten his phallus and so she commissioned one to be made of gold and with her magic conceived a falcon-headed god, god of kings, magicians, and healers. To pray to her, call her, "all that has been, and is, and shall be," call her, "Mother, mistress of all elements, primordial child of time, queen of the dead, the single manifestation of all gods and goddess that are." Nod to the shining heights of heaven. Nod to the wholesome sea breezes.

—

For a month all I can listen to is "Isis" by Bob Dylan, "The

Downeaster 'Alexa' " by Billy Joel, and "Stronger" by Kanye West. I listen to these three songs on repeat all day. There is something wrong with me, I know it. I haven't mourned correctly, but who knows how these rituals are performed? What is the prayer for a lover you've fallen out of love with and then sent to rehab, whose clothes are still in your apartment while you are newly in love with another who brings new music into your old life? He plays you the album *Mermaid Avenue,* he plays you Old Crow Medicine Show, and this sound track shifts your mummified internal tunes. And then one night you see the ghost of your old lover, the one who is supposed to be in rehab, wandering the parking lot of your apartment complex (you are listening to Billy Joel on your headphones, "The Downeaster 'Alexa' " drilling through your ear canals), and he looks at you and you don't know if you should make eye contact with a spirit, but when you look up he's gone. I don't know how to preform these rites properly. I don't have enough faith, or maybe I have too many gods, having borrowed everything that made me shimmer with hope and applied it to my aching heart. I'm sick or healing, dying, or being reborn. I run to purify myself. I do yoga in the steam shower. I crave sweat like water.

—

What are you listening to? my high school poetry teacher demanded. *Crap. Crap.* He said. *You are all listening to crap. Your assignment is to write out the lyrics of a Bob Dylan song onto something, your body, a wall, a pizza box, until he becomes the very sound track of your life,* until you make mix tapes with nothing but different versions of "Tangled Up in Blue," until you can sing his part to Johnny Cash's "North Country Fair," until you see yourself on that highway in the rain, separating from a young lover, until you are that woman, until you marry him like Isis and he leaves you and then returns and you write his words on a poster, until you see him play once in the rain as an old man you can barely understand yet his words are your scripture.

—

It's my favorite vision of Dylan: 1979 and he's been electric for over a decade and he's confident in front of the band. They call it the Rolling Thunder Revue, and they'll tour in the fall and spring, bringing Joan Baez, Roger McGuinn, and Ramblin' Jack Elliot along, recording a live concert album, *The Bootleg Series Vol. 5.* In the video of a performance of "Isis," Dylan's given up playing anything but his harmonica. He's skinny and mystical, wearing a big brown hat with flowers and feathers in the brim. Under the deep shadow of the stage lights occasionally his clear blue eyes flash like sapphires, almost too cold. His curls are tight from sweat, salt, tears. He's got on a vest and a long scarf and he's painted his face with some sort of white paint, something primitive and chalky, so he looks sick and powerful and otherworldly in the blue lights of the stage. When he sings he looks off as if he's focused on something we can't see. He's out questing through pyramids and ice, jolting to the sound of the band, to the screaming of the violin. His Isis is just beyond reach, waiting in a meadow to be awakened by love.

—

What is the formula for dividing two lives? When two young poets buy a book together in a used bookstore in Taos and their hands smell like the same bed, the same cigarettes, whose book is it three years later? Is it his because he wrote poetry while she wrote essays? Or is it hers because Whitman was a poet of earth and sprout and she was always the grounded one, while her lover was a writer of air and hauntings, when *please, let's be practical* was her chant as their relationship was breaking apart and he was crying for *drugs and dark painted rooms and Paris?* Usually I am good

at sorting things, putting objects in boxes, text on lines, but I have
to weigh each book out like I'm judging a soul. Books were, after
all, the bones of our love, and even if I was bitter to him and tired
of that love, I still respect those bound words. I give him Neruda
and Jeffers, I give him Vallejo, too, along with most of the Snyder
and all of the Dylan Thomas. I keep Mary Oliver, Donald Hall;
they are the foundation stones in my house of the mind. And then
my hands find the burlap-bound edition of *Leaves of Grass*, dark
green, musty smelling, bigger than any other poetry volume, as
if it needed a larger page to exclaim its joy. I hold its rough cover
to my breast, yellowed paper, broken spine, and though we used
to read it out loud to each other, I know it is mine. Deep in the
ground there is Whitman. I break the book open over my knee
and read a verse to empower me as I split our apartment in two,
packing his things, leaving mine. Each exclamation point is an
espresso shot, a sunrise! My body grows stronger and I feel blood,
skin, hair, animal, electric again.

DURGA

She was born fully grown and perfect. The male gods who found
themselves powerless to fight a buffalo demon made her from their
collective energies, so that she was all of them and greater still, and
to her they bowed and gave their sacred weapons. Mounted on a
tiger, she received them calmly, with her legs crossed, holding a
weapon in each of her eight arms: the chakra, conch, bow, arrow,
sword, javelin, shield, and trident. One of her eyes is the moon.
The other is the sun. The middle eye, between her dark brows, is a
raging fire. Her name means "fort"; her name means "invincible."
Mountain goddess. Earth goddess. Goddess of war, she is beyond
reach, first of all who merit worship. Durga created the world at
her will, and she dwells in everything. Sometimes she holds a pen

and scrolls; a stylus is her weapon. Dance and sing for her and immerse yourself in water. Pray to her for protection from bad dreams and omens, to remove obstacles, to calm a restless, fearful baby, to destroy your enemies, to increase prosperity. She is the savior of women and protector of men. Take a shower, wash with rose water, face north, bow on a red cloth, lay out a fresh flower . . . now, with all sincerity, ask her to grant you the desire of your life, in your own language, for she understands all tongues. Close your eyes and concentrate.

—

My new lover practices yoga and I ask him to hold his hands in reverse prayer pose, bound low behind his back while I sketch him. I ask him to take eagle arms and I snap pictures so I can draw from them later. His tattooed arms contorted, his hands placed back to back. He is knotted magically, so tight I want to tease them out, one finger at a time, until they're wrapped around me. When I take the same poses I wonder if I feel like he does in them. Bound up in knots, my hands reach high, muscle pulled tight, joints twisted. This is what it feels like to be stuck. This is what it feels like to be free.

—

Yoga is my college PE elective and it's held in the same basement studio where last semester I took women's self defense and learned to yell "fire!" instead of "help!" and to kick men in the balls and break a nose with the back of my hand. There is a mirror but the yoga teacher sets us up facing away from it. We begin by holding a finger to a nostril and controlling our breath. Then we meditate. Our assignment is to read through a list of suggested mantras and to memorize one for next week. I choose to chant to Durga, *Om Sri durgayai namah,* a goddess with eight arms loaded with weapons, riding a tiger. She looks like a woman I'd like on my side and her name sounds like a deep earthy spice; it rolls on my tongue, it tastes like iron.

ARJUMAND BANU BEGUM

At thirteen she was betrothed to Shah Jahan, a prince two years her senior who had heard of her wit and had read her Persian poems. She was warm and confident and was painted, always, holding a rose between her pointer finger and thumb. At eighteen she married Shah Jahan, and after their wedding celebration he gave her a new name, Mumtaz Mahal, or Exalted One of the Palace, and their marriage was one of love so grand the court poets sang of their intimacy, affection, and eroticism. When he became Emperor, she became Queen of the World, Queen of the Age. Her palace was decorated with pure gold and precious stones and had rose water fountains where she might dip her small, sweet feet. To him she bore fourteen children, and to her he gave his imperial seal with which she forgave enemies and commuted death sentences. They stayed up late playing chess. They loved their children. He took her to the battlefield for advice. She died delivering their fourteenth child. Her body was buried temporarily in a walled pleasure garden on the banks of an old river on the outskirts of the kingdom where the couple had been traveling. After her death, Shah Jahan went into seclusion for a year. When he reappeared, coaxed back to court by his eldest daughter, he was bent and white of hair. He ordered Mumtaz's body disinterred and carried in a golden casket back to Agra, where he began designing her mausoleum, a building as feminine as his beloved, with curved domes and graceful calligraphy inlaid with gemstones. Twenty thousand men labored on the site for two decades. Why it is named the Taj Mahal no one can remember. Mumtaz's cenotaph sits in the very center of the great domed inner chamber, and beneath that, in a modest crypt, her husband's tomb rests besides hers. On the lid of her casket, a sculpted writing tablet. On the lid of his, a pen.

—

Yoga is a series of postures preformed repetitively, like a dance. After a few weeks of class I know them by heart. I buy a mat so I can practice in my apartment, so I can flow from pose to pose without having to look up for guidance. Before I begin the physical practice, I focus on breathing, I chant the mantra to Durga. I let things slip away until the mat is the only part of the world that remains, an island in the messy apartment that I am splitting down the middle. Yoga is the only hour of silence in my day, no music to guide or empower me, no electric guitars to push me, just the beating of my heart and breath through my lungs, skin on mat, skin on skin, my hair brushing my face.

—

On Friday mornings I create a ritual. I wake early and head to the community center gym across the parking lot. I run on the treadmill, watching the day's news unthread on the screen before me, its text ticker repeating like a fabric's pattern. Then, naked, I enter the steam sauna where I stretch and spread long on the tile between the wooden seats. The water fills me and expands me. My pores open, I towel off and dart back across the lot to my apartment where I take the longest shower of the week. I wash my hair deeply. I shave up high on my legs and carefully under my arms and tap the razor clean under the faucet. I am getting ready to see my new boyfriend, although I'll have to wait through three history classes and drive two hours north before I stand at his threshold. He'll open the door to me, and there I'll be changed, a woman polished, a woman purified. As I get dressed I picture myself standing before him, then the image settles deeper as I blow dry my hair, my head tipped over, filling with blood. I see myself through my own eyes, not through his. Each lock braided, knotted in place. Eyeliner sharp as a bird's markings. My dress holding me gently and, underneath, my limbs renewed through yoga, through steam and water, so that I am almost made again. I can feel the expansion just beneath the surface of myself. On Friday mornings I wake before my alarm with something shifting in my veins, electric. Rebirth is a betrayal of the old image as much it is a new creation. I've crossed out her picture. I've learned a new song.

—

I ask my new boyfriend to come to a lecture at my college about the Taj Mahal. India runs through our love, a ghost flavor, almost like another woman. He's traveled the country often and has a picture of her busy streets taped to the wall of his bedroom. I gaze at it from our nest of blankets on the floor. He runs to the memory of India when he needs to feel grounded, when his mind slips and his eyes turn gray. In India everything is bright and toxic and he feels, he says, truly alive. I am jealous of her because I am not so exotic; if I were a place, I would be our hometown in New Hampshire, I would be white pine, stone wall, barn board, maple syrup: dark in summer, snow white in winter. See, she has all the mystery. I try to love her too, for his sake. During the lecture we sit with our hands bound together but I look at him looking at the slides and wonder where he's off to. He looks a little like T. E. Lawrence, and I imagine my lover in robes and loose pants, trying to blend into the crowds of Mumbai. There are so many ways shape shift.

—

After the semester ends I continue yoga classes with my teacher at her home studio across town. She lives in a brightly painted

Craftsman-style home where she's renovated her small basement. To get there, I have to walk through her back garden. Up against the house, near the entrance to the studio, there are old bookshelves lined with plugged-in heat blankets where the cats can sleep on chilly nights. A rough, old, orange tomcat and two curled-together kittens greet me the first day I take a class. My teacher is gray haired, full figured, and goddess beautiful. She emits a joyful energy. She hangs scarves and jewels off her body like altar offerings; she moves feline and sensual but laughs earth-honest, and her teeth are stained and imperfect. Her hands on my body when she helps me correct or deepen a pose, warm beyond normal human heat. I wonder at her; I study her and ask which road leads to such power?

—

My new lover and I are driving back from the high desert toward Portland. The Cascades range ahead of us, ethereal in sunset, the peaks luminous as planets. Through the dark plain, wild horses kick up dust at the edges of the world. He's driving, and, sitting in the passenger seat, I feel a great poem rise up inside of me, like nausea, like something winged caged, so I grab the handout from the Taj Mahal lecture and use my thigh muscles as a table. I write in the darkness, with only the feel of the pen's point as my guide, a poem about the whole continent behind us, and the great Pacific ahead over the crest of the mountains. I write about high school dances and empty parking lots and forests of white pine where the light from kitchen windows is spilling over blackberry bramble and onto old barn board, and meadows where women are napping. I write about prisons and the expanse of highway ribbon's freedom, and horses, because I've seen them just now, wild beyond the barbed wire, and I love both old and new but all from the same source like a great river birthed from glaciers at the top of the world, and a woman who is so beautiful her grave is visited by two million people a year, and electric plants along the shores of Lake Erie, and a phone line crackling. But the next day when I look at it the poem is nothing, just scribbles, written too quickly and too blindly to be read. I held it for years as if I might somehow divine my lines or at least absorb their power and transfer them to other poems. It remained a singular mystery, and I must have, one day, moving or cleaning out my desk, crumbled it into the recycling. The energy is what matters after all, the flood of it. I remember that I could be both pen and paper.

—

I wake early to bright light from the East. The apartment is stale to me, this mess on the floor of boxes and books, so I roll my yoga mat up and walk across the street to the community center gym. *Is there a quiet place I can practice?* I ask the woman behind the front desk, and she unlocks the dance studio just for me, this early weekday morning. The space is honey pine and high lacquer, high ceilinged with beams like whalebones, a wall of mirrors reflecting light upon light. I set myself central, my mat a small island, my body a long shadow on the walls. I face myself in the mirrors as I meditate and, rising, see my body from straight on. I study it honestly like an artist surveying a model, I note its symmetry and where one shoulder sits high and one hip low, I note the amber-brown eyes, the sleek dark hair, ink in the skin of my foot and curling around my waist. I move through the poses as I move in the mirror as I move in the shadow. I am my own dance partner, and perhaps it's this fissure of forms from the singular to the plural, but suddenly, and for the first time with real clarity, I love myself. I inhale the smell of my skin, the salt of sweat, the pungent inside-body smell of my breath, the sweetness of hair, and when I come back to myself through steady inhales, lying on my mat in the center of the floor, I am intoxicated with myself.

The Fox

WE WERE IN THE CABIN by the river. There were candles inside and on the porch, but the moon was bright. It was the end of June, that green time when the world was full. The farm was beautiful then, all of our promises were unbroken. The world was neat, the lines straight just like we intended them. Our dock headed out into the river, with purpose, like a raised hand. The river ran around and under, brown and slick with moonlight. It made no noise. A thick mist had settled on the fields. It sat near to the ground like a fallen cloud. It sank low and made sounds travel strangely. It looked like smoke or gunfire from old wars. It was a little scary, like something that you would disappear into, like a monster itself, with an ever-changing form, something that swallowed people, trees, and fields and left them emptied of their souls. The mists rolled and fell down the hills to the river.

There was a fire by the water. Sometimes we stood by it. Sometimes we sat on the picnic tables outside the cabin. Sometimes we sat in the cabin. Those were our stations. We were all drunk. We'd known each other for years and were very comfortable in our drunkenness. We didn't hide it, and we didn't try to dress it up and make it friendly or funny or entertaining. These nights took us different places. Often we got there together, we'd construct a car and a journey and travel there all at once, like there was no individual say in the matter. Mostly we were all the same in our drinking. All headed down the same path. This was a high point; these were the good times before the real problems, before the things that happened that made us get sober. These were the times we wished we could have stayed in, the friendly, happy nights, settled down in the fun, the pleasure of sharing yourself, drunk, with people you love and who are like you.

We each had our methods, and they remained the same. I drank wine. I liked the taste of it more, the drunk like a fleece blanket covered in heavy novels. The guys drank beer. Max started with a big bottle of microbrew, a first course, and then followed it with cans of Molson Canadian. Ryan liked to drink from bottles, Budweisers, or pounders of PBR. Callie took a bottle of white wine out of her fridge and nursed it all night; she got drunk fast and fell asleep. She was Max's wife, and this was her weekend. During the week, she was clean and sober, unlike the three of us, who filled our evenings with drinking and talking and planning the farm's future. Colin drank beer first then whiskey. His eyes got pink like a rabbit's. He fell in love with everyone and everything. He sang and played the guitar; he could make me cry when he sang. Ryan, Max ,and I smoked. We'd buy a pack each at the store. Yellow boxes of American Spirits. Sometimes it was just a chance to smoke. We were trying to quit. We were always trying to quit.

It was a time of the night with no time. We had forgotten dinner. We had lost the chance to go home and sleep in our beds like normal people. We knew that rest if it came, would be somewhere uncomfortable, in the bed of a truck, on the futon in the cabin, the grass on the lawn, Max and Callie's couch, or maybe in a lawn chair. That night with the rolling fog we were all traveling to a place that was dark. We'd decided on this somehow. We wanted to pick our scabs. We wanted to bleed again.

One by one we told each other the stories of our parent's abuse, physical or otherwise. We shared them in a circle, formally, like we are at a meeting. I told them that I was spanked, often because I was a mean kid with a bad mouth. I was sent to my room without dinner. The spanking didn't hurt, but it was incredibly embarrassing. I remembered the shame of having my pants pulled down by my father. I remembered my stomach rolling at that. My mother slapped me when I was a teenager. I slapped her back. I was never the daughter she wanted. I got away with everything in high school because I became an excellent liar; I hid, snuck around, and withheld everything. If they knew, they never asked. If there were rules, I worked around them so much that I don't remember having rules.

I was seventeen when I first wanted to get drunk, not just tipsy like I'd get at parties. I had a friend buy me a bottle of vodka. I called my boyfriend, Ian, he lived in Colorado, and we talked, and I told him that I was going to drink until I passed out. I was going to tell him how many shots I had, as I took them. I put on sexy lingerie. Drinking made me feel hot, like a girl who did whatever. One, two, three, four, five. I kept going until time became elastic and black. Ian told me that I made it to thirteen before I dropped the phone. He hung up eventually on my blank line. I woke up with vomit on my pillow. There was vomit on the floor in the bathroom and on the toilet. I remembered thinking that it was someone else's, maybe my sister's. I thought maybe I had eaten something bad. I cleaned it all up. I took a shower; I washed it out of my hair. I felt heavy; I had a headache so I lay on the lawn in my bikini sunbathing for the rest of the day. I didn't connect anything. The vomit to the vodka, the shots to the dull black headache. The missing time in the night when I had dropped the phone and gone into a mute conversation with the world.

Mostly I felt, at all times, that I needed to improve and to be the best at everything, the most beautiful, the best in school, the most responsible. I kept everything else in the dark. I had good parents, a nice home. My story, I thought, wasn't very good. It was mostly about me lying. It was about my shame at being spanked. How it punished nothing and only made me realize the importance of good lies. Good lies got me out of the shame. Good lies made me better.

We went around in our circle sharing these things. The drinks in our hands pulled us closer, like magnets. The fog rolled through our night, changing everything. It revealed parts of the landscape briefly and then covered it again. The full moon's brightness made it more haunting, revealing our ritual that should have taken place in the dark. It was so luminous that we could see each tree in the hedgerow, each letter on our license plates, the edges of the road and end of the rows in the field. Almost daylight but pale, the moon as high as the sun at midday, casting its own, weak shadows, black on gray

Max was last to tell his story. He was, as always, the drunkest of us. He couldn't hold his head up really. It rolled between his shoulders. *I mean, fuck it*, he said, *fuck it, all this bullshit, all the times I was spanked and slapped. With rulers. Fuck it.* We tried to follow him. The divorce that split his life between two places, summers in Wisconsin, school years in Vermont. His father's sad little place, where he was left spooning Chef Boyardee out of cans or eating frozen pizzas frozen, scanning cable channels all day while his father was at work. Meeting his father's new girlfriend, the secretary that he cheated on his mom with, their awkward dinners out at family restaurants.

The words came slowly, or all together. He started to cry. We all started to cry. At pain and the memory of pain. It felt like the right thing to do, a sign of respect, or understanding. There wasn't any stopping it. It was where the night was taking us. We cried.

We had another drink. We lit cigarettes and the light showed the tears on our cheeks. We didn't look at each other. We felt ourselves winding down like rocket shells, falling back to earth. All the air was gone, the fuel burnt, the pain turning the booze black inside, weighing down our eyelids.

Max stood up and held onto the porch railing, like a man on a ship's deck in a big storm. He led himself to the stairs. He sat there. I pulled myself out of the dark water and slunk toward him, all hips, my feet trying to find a line in front of me. I sat next to him. We looked out at the fog. We looked out at the moonlight on the fog, highlighting it like stage lighting as it rolled and formed and covered the things we knew so well. He took a flashlight from his belt and scanned the fog. He drew it back and forth, searching for something, trying to find what was below or in or behind it.

The light caught on two eyes. He stood up. *What the fuck*, he said. A fox sat at the edge of the field, deliberately seated, watching us. It could have been there all night. Its grace betrayed nothing of its intent. *What the fuck are you doing?* Max asked the fox. *What the fuck are you doing watching us?* The fox's ears moved a bit, but it remained. Its eyes hit bright in the flashlight. Max started crying. He stood up, holding onto the railing. He was breathing heavily. *I'm going to fucking kill that thing. What the fuck is it doing? Go away! What are you looking at?*

I thought he was trying to walk to his truck and get his pistol or his rifle but he couldn't move and just sank onto the step again, his head in his hands, defeated by the booze. His crying rocked the whole world.

When I looked back toward the field, the fox was gone. Its tail bobbed down the road along the river. Had it been it hunting, hungry, watching us, waiting for us to die, to poison ourselves. Had it thought maybe if it stayed there a little while longer we would become carrion? Had it been learning from us, from our circle, our steady pace between river, porch and cabin, like good animals, predictable and cyclical? Had it heard crying before and recognized something familiar in it, as its screams in the night? There was something unnerving about being watched by that animal as we self-destructed, as we broke into small, simple pieces. Our human selves were becoming wounded, wild things, falling from grace like gunshot snow geese.

Max was crying and crying and muttering about killing the fox. *Its fine*, I said. *Its just a fox.*

We didn't let things pass like that, unburdened. The fog was not just fog. It was death. It was a truer night than the night itself. The moonlight was more than a star's light reflected from a heavenly body, our bodies weren't just bodies, they were vessels. We made cuts into scars that reminded us to continue those practices, to keep crafting those stories in which we would never win.

I found my way up to Max and Callie's couch in the dark, through the fog, through the landscape I thought I knew. I walked counter to the world. I said, *fuck it, fuck you.* How could the things that hurt us define us more than the things that we love? The fox, the watcher in the night, who was drawn to our pain like the smell of blood, our cries like the cries of things wounded, and ready to die. He was waiting for the grace that would not come to us, the grace we didn't deserve.

The Coolest Monsters

I LIVED FOR A SEASON on an island connected to the mainland by a long causeway. Rocks were piled up along the road to build it further out of the sea, but I waited for the day when the water would rise and cut us off. I worked at a general store that had been in business for two hundred years. The place was thick with memory and visited on tidal cycles by lobster men who needed sandwiches, coffee, newspapers, and beers. When there were no customers the store made its own noises, happily, like a woman at home all day. I walked to work past a cemetery where men lost at sea were laid to rest, or, at least, their names were, their bodies drifted elsewhere in the hugeness of the ocean. Their memories were pinned there, as if to keep the current from sweeping them out further, held down by the metal crosses and granite head-stones. I feared that ground, empty under the scattered memorials and would hold my breath as I walked by. You could dig into it, and it would be just as a field or a plot in the forest, free from bone and coffin lid. A place for mourning, for sorrow, for resting, an empty box. It scared me that people invented what didn't exist. They took their ghosts and planted them to grow out their own stories, selfishly, while the real flesh spun into a deep eddies between continents.

During the World Wars, sailors hoped that tattoos would identify their bodies if they were dredged up, bloated, terribly white and blue, wiped out to sea by water or fire. A bit of skin would be seen by a man who had been a brother or friend and instead of being MIA they would be declared dead. No hope, just the final grace of certainty. I've covered my arms and legs, my lower back with ink, carved up my flesh with needles. I remember my blood on paper towels, blood turning Vaseline pink, blood dark with ink, and healing, how my body wanted so badly to scar over, to force out the image. Only my right leg is naked; the rest of me would have to be skinned to hide who I had been. I want to know that I'll be known, by someone, naked in life and naked in death. My body speaks for me, retelling its own myths, remembering the dream of a woman, *the hawk, the eagle, the girl in the field.*

—

Viking berserkers slashed their tongues with knives before storming the beaches of northern islands, lands like snowdrifts in the surf. The adrenaline fueled their sacred rage, and they became the wolf-spirit, the small hero, a human with humanity bled out. They opened their eyes too wide, so all the white showed and stuck out their slashed tongues, dripping blood, feeding on what others created, they became the huge wolf packs of those broad shores, the beasts that cry in the darkness of a night too cold to remember when even the moon forgets the good times. I stuck out my tongue for my boyfriend, Ian, the one with a body like a Greek statue, shaped by kick boxing classes in the suburbs of Colorado Springs, and he drew the razor over my tongue, or up it, or across it. The fear of it being cut side to side, the fear of it being severed down the middle like a snake. The fear of sharp metal in the mouth.

The fear of flavorless, mute futures like drooling, mad children, falling from my lips. Never to speak or taste or sing. Opening for him, love and fear mixing like water and blood. My cut tongue so bright, that impossible reaction of body and atmosphere. The terror of pain and the terror at the rise, the blood, darkening the corners of everything, wondering, *what am I capable of?*

—

Early in the spring along the old roads of New England the sound of sap striking the buckets rings from tree to tree. A ping like someone plucking a tight string of cat gut. The rhythm picking up pace as the day heats, like a heartbeat rising in fear. At three o'clock, when the sun rests high up in the empty canopies the sap runs wildly, losing all rhyme, it rushes; it runs itself desperately into the galvanized steel. The taps are drilled into the great veins that feed into separation of trunk and limb, and the maple men find them like surgeons, beginning at the base, where snow still piles and then follow the bark lines upward. One tap for the young trees, four or five or six on the oldest maples, each their allotted blood draw, they give what they can without dying. There is a special bit for cutting the tree, different from screwing or biting into a wall. They knock the tap into the raw hole, the metal needle, stuck with a hook at one end from which the bucket is hung. The trees, coming to life, moving water from their roots to their crowns again, remembering upward movement, remembering blooming and the great storms of spring. At the tap they are drawn out, their clear blood just slightly sweet. Their draining becomes the music of spring, horrible and excited. At death the boards of the old sugar maples bear the bite marks, the scars of all their years of service, like needle holes on the arm, circling the trunk. Decades of pain, of stunted growth all for sugar, for the tongue's pleasure in the condensed snowmelt the tree made for itself, for its own life.

—

The day I was brave enough to ask to be set free I sat on his bed looking at the tiles. I held my legs to my chest like a life vest. He agreed to break up but if the radio played a Rolling Stones song, he said we had to stay together. In silence, we waited, and "Wild Horses" ran through the speakers, sad and true. The great beasts throwing their manes into a mystical sunset along the ridge lines in the Old West like beautiful, naked women. He smiled at fate, his power that seemed almost impossible; like he was the god he hoped to be. "Wild Horses" rushed in and licked the salt from the tear rivers on my cheeks with their huge, rough tongues. I rested my brow on their narrow foreheads; their big eyelashes brushed against my ears. Bareback, unbroken they left me there, looking at the tile, interested in my grief only briefly in the kind, quick curiosity of wild things, the things that find hurt in hurt, joy in joy.

—

Swans came to the lake that year. Much bigger than any bird I had seen up close, white as snow banks in the moonlight. They shattered into their own reflections on the cold dark lake, they broke through their quivering swan-mirror and landed in the ripples of that form, swimming in white swan reflection, floating above the frozen bodies of cars, men, hungry northern fish, sunken shanties, snowmobiles, and trucks. I watched them from the beach in the last hours of light, wrapped in my jacket against late autumn's almost winter cold. The kind boy from my history class, Jason, sat beside me, always without his coat like he ran hotter than everyone else. *What element would you be,* he asks. I think of them all, fire, water, earth, air, their powers and truths, the women who each would be. *I would be air,* I say watching the swans beat the currents upwards with their wings. They were created for rising, created for beating against the strongest force in the world, as if even planets, physics, or the weight of the atmosphere was nothing but the desire to be above, to see the world flattened, to be just a little part of everything, better, more beautiful than all of it.

—

In the woods at sugaring time, I meet him again after many years. Robert, the boy who dragged my heart around, the boy I returned to as if returning was its own virtue. I think of one of the men killed in the Salem witch trials sentenced to be crushed to death. His punishment was slower than the rest. Increasingly heavy stones were laid on his chest while he looked up into the clear sky. I imagine it, the sky of spring through bare trees. At each stone, he was asked to confess to the impossible, the summoning of spirits, spirits that bring love or kill our enemies with just a drop of blood and a poem. He said no until the last stone broke his ribs, the bones punched through his lungs, and he drowned in his own blood. Each time we meet the stones gets heavier. Robert and I walk up into the deep heart of the woods. Love, love sits at the tip of my tongue like the taste of blood. On the way back to the sugar house I find a wasp nest woven onto milkweed, dried and swaying top-heavy in the snowmelt field. With my pocket knife, I cut into it and reveal each layer, the sleeping wasps, the chambers of their hearts, their home made from spit, spun in the hot mouth of summer. It looks like a doll house, the children in their bedrooms, the mother in the kitchen, the father in the living room, the cars in the garage. Frozen, either dead or sleeping, I don't know.

—

All the scars on my ankles and my inner arms are gone now. I used to be able to see them in the summer; they never grew as dark as the other skin. I used to fear the knives in their drawers, the scissors' blades, the razor living in the mouth of the box cutter. I see him, Ian, yellow-haired, fatter now sometimes. Facebook suggests him as someone I may know. I still imagine killing him. These dreams used to keep me busy when I lay in fear at night, like counting sheep I ran them over and over again. He would be in the hospital recovering from some routine surgery, like appendicitis, and I would walk in, dressed like a nurse, in the strange quiet hours of the hospital when Death reads all the worn magazines in the waiting rooms and drinks out of the fountains like a tall dog with thumbs and a long tongue. My heels would click down the hallway, neat as Nazi's boots, and I would slip a needle of poison into his IV and watch him choke on his own blood, fizzing like reddened dish soap bubbles. Or I would park a motorcycle outside a bar some place where the plains meet the mountains. The machine would shake silently between my legs. Wearing tight leather and soft jeans I'd push through the glass door into the sort of bar where no one pays attention to you, everyone drowning slowly like rats in a bucket. Nobody turns as I draw a sword from my back and cut through his neck as he sits, facing the alter of lit bottles, arranging peanut shells like tarot cards so that as his head falls it lands chin first on the bar, looking deeply into his peanut shell prophecy. The coolest monster, the woman who brings death. Kali, with her tongue bleeding onto her breasts, she will kill the whole world unless she is stopped by her beloved Krishna, his body pressed to the earth under her feet, the weight of the skulls around her waist crushing him. *Stop, stop,* he pleads, and she lets the lust run from her like animals fleeing a forest on fire, like swans flying ahead of the white cold of winter, and becomes woman again, a lover, a mother, a girl.

＿

In the witching hour, all the monsters walk under the sky. Men become wolves. Women ride in the sky on brooms, in cauldrons, on wings that have sprouted from their backs. The dead rise and return to the places they loved. They touch plow handles. They stand at windows looking out, having let themselves in. They feel for the ghost bodies of ghost pets. Dead horses rise in their strength from their grave behind the barn, tossing their heads again in the painful light of the moon. The oldest dark things, the beasts and clouds of evil, lick at their lipless mouths with bloody tongues. Their many eyes roll toward the bright eye in the sky; they feel their power roar red in their skulls. This is the hour that I have to creep downstairs to use my bathroom. I am so scared that I stay in bed for as long as I can. I can hear the cold breaking at the fragile parts of the world. The trees popping as their veins explode with the frost, their vertical rivers shattering into ice crystals. The floors bite under my feet. Downstairs the windows stare like open eyes. I don't want to look out and see what I know I will see. This fear radiates like the warmth of a fire; I can feel it pulse and move in the wind. The pilot light on the stove burns away, unnoticed during the day when there are brighter lights. It glows blue around the edges, it burns for burning because it always has to be on, awake when everything else is in the off position, a watcher, guardian of the hearth, of waking. Blue as the eye of a baby. I stare into it, I have never noticed it before. Blue like a sapphire ring-stone, or a wildflower, that rare color of peace, it settles in my heart, burning.

—

I was always terrified of the graveyard of those lost at sea. The graveyard was about grief, about cuts that are picked over and over until they scar. Until the scar becomes the thing, the reminder, the pain made fresh each time, that gasp at the cut itself, the blood and its taste, sweet, salty, so bright that you wonder at your own hidden beauty, your oceans. But without pins, without places to hold them they follow me, like the ghosts of children, and I their mother, wandering through the corners of my futures. They ask me about the cuts; they want to know where the scars came from. Why I would let someone do those things, *was it the pain, did it feel good?* Pulling them off my skirts I look each of them in the eyes. I dig shallow graves in my heart-desert and bury them alive so that the last thing they say is *sand*, is *earth*. I leave them unmarked. Coming back to this country I hope to remember only that they are buried there. I hope not to remember where, in case I want to kneel before them, leave a handful of blue flowers, water them with tears and from them grow again something that tastes like blood and looks like a dog of a child, with a huge tongue and eyes like the moon in winter.

Dear Meriwether Lewis

I.

IN YOUR DREAMS THE COUNTRY becomes a map with the hand-drawn waterways like a surgeon's guide to the body, up country, downstream, all following the easiest path. The mountains rise and again you are trapped in the snowy gulches and deep-throated avalanche channels. You at the mouth of the Columbia, where I've read there are more waterfalls then anywhere else in the world, great corridors fall down into that river, steep and tough in the north and choked with a mist that breaks through the spruce and cedar at the coast. You are there at the edge of everything, camped for the wet season in a shingled fort, the rain in your bones and in the blue of your wrist veins. You trace them up the forearm, to that soft spot in the elbow and then up through your shoulder across the breast bone to where they pool and pulse. There is nothing to do but return, with your bags filled with specimens, the shining birds and prairie creatures, gutted and eyeless.

2.

I am trying to remember the details, trying to construct a history of our love story from the facts only, upward to something grander, a guide perhaps, or a map. We spent the afternoon stopping at all the little waterfalls, following their path down to where they broke on slabs of dark rock, the water flowing, whole again, under the road and down into the greater river. At the top there was a bridge and we stood there watching everything fall beneath our feet. Robert said he didn't like heights, he'd never told me that before, but I have always liked that feeling of the stomach coming up through the throat, leaning just past gravity. We couldn't say anything because the water was so loud. We kissed in the broken mist of the first terrace, the water droplets hanging off my lashes. His eyes were the color of the wet rock, the sort that becomes dull and flat when it dries but is always kept slick and slate blue by the falls.

3.

In the history books they show you on a rise above the plains, in leather and uniform with a breeze from the Continental Divide blowing the fringe on your jacket back toward the Mississippi. You squint into the western sun, like some great bird, just ahead of Clark with his sunburned skin and heavy forearms. I have always imagined you right before you put a bullet in your head. The intake of breath like the storms first tracking up valley, the eyes closed, finding the temple like a surgeon with the gun barrel, the teeth set, and outside in that hotel the other people drinking and falling asleep without terror, and the country filling in all the places that were only waterways and mountain ranges on your maps and all of their quick starts at the sound of the gun while you faded, backwards through increasing darkness, up to the spring source where the purest water rises.

On the Island

THE ISLAND HOUSE IS NOT what I am expecting. It's far bigger and more formal, and I am suddenly very aware that I haven't packed right. We stopped on the drive down to pick up lemons. His mother texted us that she needed them. I bought a bouquet of sunflowers and wrapped them again so they didn't look store-bought. The island itself is not what I had imagined, all the years that I've known Robert and heard his stories about their house on Cape Cod. I'd pictured something like their house in our home-town, maybe a little rougher around the edges since it was a sec-ond home.

In Etna, New Hampshire, they live at the top of an open field in a gray cape. It's two houses really, a small log cabin where his parents had lived when they were first married, in a sort of hunting camp that had been given to them as a wedding present. After Robert was born they added a new house to the sidewall of the cabin, a simple saltbox with a granite step that always held the warmth of the sun long past dusk. They filled the home with antiques that weren't just ornaments, rolling pins oiled with lard and smoothed by genera-tions of women, the Nazi rifles his grandfather, a pediatrician, was given as payment by a poor veteran after treating his sick child. Everything has a lived-in history, and a connection to the town.

Their family names mark the streets that they live on. It is a deep, comfortable home, deliberately unfussy, as beautiful as a tomboy in her high school summers, freckled and tanned.

They have an old barn in whose corners we found treasures as kids, old pull saws, and litters of tiny, soft kittens with blue eyes. The light fell through the barn, filtered through the wide cracks between the sideboards, stretched and warped with the weathering years. Dust became gold, light became angels. That's what we called them, these thick yellow rays that illuminated old hay, a decaying pickup truck, our own thin limbs like we were being blessed. Robert's father hays their broad fields; he tends to the cows and the garden, he cuts and stacks wood for the winter. He retired from the town's fire department, the main one with ladder trucks and bunk beds but still volunteered at the small station in Etna. He keeps his boots and overalls in the corner of their bedroom, stiff, holding their form as if a ghost filled them. Robert's mother teaches third grade. In the summers, the whole family left for weeks to go to the Cape. I would say goodbye to Robert and miss our days with the barn angels and kittens. I would write him letters posted to a Massachusetts address.

I imagined the letters arrived at a place that smelled like a boathouse, damp, and piney, with a rough porch and grassy dunes. I imagined a fire pit on the beach, an old canoe or Sunfish, speckled with black mold. A kitchen with sticky linoleum, a fridge covered with pictures from the last decade, the boys all knees and sunburns with their white-blond hair, their little sister always the princess, held up, carried. They called her Wendy like they were the lost boys in Peter Pan and she was their savior, their little mother.

That weekend we'd been offered the bed in the downstairs suite. His mother thought that maybe we would want some privacy. I agreed with her. We are twenty-two and about to leave each other for school, having both transferred for our fall semesters. We make plans about seeing each other, visiting on weekends but we don't know, we've broken up before, we've come together again, too; I don't know how long we can keep doing it like this. All these questions are making me sick. I cry for nights, or during the middle of a drive somewhere, anything can set me off. I hope to spend the mornings together, slowly waking in bed, the light clean over the white sheets and the folds of our bodies. I dreamed of those nights on the Cape, our skin salty and dark from the beach, the salt on my tongue, rough on our arms. I hope to make memories so sweet that I can feed off them for years, nursing the heartbreak that I can sense coming, like the air shifting before a storm.

But his grandmother died this spring, just a few months ago, and Robert doesn't feel that it's right to take what had been her room. So the big suite downstairs, with a king-size bed and floor-to-ceiling windows sits empty this weekend, open to the ghosts of the previous generation. I feel robbed of the moments I want with him, as if those memories, somehow are already mine. I'm angry with him for not understanding but I held him after his grandmother's funeral and watched him cry for the first time at her death and also feel ashamed at my bitterness. I want to be bigger than my needs; I think that would make him stay.

We move our bags upstairs to one of the little bedrooms with bunk beds. It's the room where he spent his childhood summers. The room is still decorated for kids. A hooked rug with blue, white, and gray shades twists inwards on itself on the floor. There are old Boy Scout manuals, books on fishing and how to survive getting lost in the woods, books on knot making and the currents off the Cape. Above the dresser a framed print of N.C. Wyeth's *The Giant* walks through the clouds of childhood summers, the little kids turning from their sand castle construction to watch a huge, primitive man pace the boiling thunderheads, rising at the edge of the horizon.

I take the top bunk, the bottom one had always been his. His brother is next door in the other room, with a friend from college and his sister is sleeping with a girl cousin down the hall. The girls have already changed and headed out to the beach, blonde and nearly identical. I climb up to the bunk; Robert gets into the bed below me, and for a few minutes we rest. I float above him like a clairvoyant lover. I try to let my darkness leave me. Light crosses the room in long lines, illuminating each book, dresser, and wallboard. Downstairs people are rattling dishes, opening and closing doors, clinking glasses, using the ice machine on the fridge. I think about the thin sundresses I had packed and my worn out sandals. They embarrass me. I try to imagine how I can make them look effortless and rich. I don't know what I wished he had told me, only that I hadn't known the truth.

The house is just too nice. It casts everything else about the family in a new way. It makes them a little less romantic, not charmed, just wealthy, that the grace of their living was not greased by luck or poetry but old bank accounts and inheritance. My family is the sort of upper middle-class that is always fighting for something, taking out loans, trying to hide old couches with new covers and spray painting over the mold on the deck furniture. I've always wondered at his family's ease, their happy schedule, so unforced, their long formal meals and weeks away in the summer. The house takes a bit of this away. I taste heartbreak as we go downstairs for dinner.

In the dining room his mother has put my grocery store sunflowers in a tall vase and centered them on the table; she is always kind to me. Robert and I sit together, elbow to elbow, and eat clams and sweet corn, green salad with jewel-like vinaigrette, and blueberry shortcake. The ladies in the family drink white wine, sweating in big glasses. The men have beers and short cups of whiskey or rum, ice cubes rumbling and shaking as they melt into the alcohol. It's always easy being with them, their bright blond faces, their freckles, and big smiles. Robert tells his story about funny road signs in Nepal and everyone laughs.

After dinner, we step outside, and Robert lays his head on my shoulder like a tired kid. I run my fingers through his hair. I cut it short accidentally, using the wrong head on the trimmers but he wasn't upset. In the dark, the sound of the surf is loud and violent. We rock like we are slow dancing in middle school over the warm stones of the patio. He lifts his face to the wind, wind that is breaking the tiny branches off the pines, coming in off the water. He is going to go fishing if that is okay. His eyes are gray and distant, caught up in a storm system that is alien to me. I let him go when his eyes are like that; there is no keeping him. He could be gone fishing or back to Nepal, Boulder, or Cairo. The wind takes him places; he becomes a kite in it.

Robert gathers his fishing gear and passes out of sight into the night. I help his mother and aunt clean up in the kitchen, running the dishes under the faucet and organizing them in the dishwasher. We top off each other's glasses of white wine. I go upstairs to use the bathroom and when I come back down they are settled into a card game on the large, soft couch in the family room. In the kitchen, Robert's father is breaking into the liquor cabinet. He isn't fishing, or playing cards with the family, he's slinking around the edges of the evening in the garage fixing something that he's broken.

When I was younger, I remember seeing piles of the empty bottles in their recycling, bottles of beer and vodka and wine. I watched Robert's parents sip wine at dinner, politely, but I knew there were empty cans of beer on the floor in their old Subaru and a garbage can in the barn that was full of beer cans, and another one in the sugar house. I never saw his father drinking. After he retired he drank during the day, when he was by himself, mowing, raking the hay, walking the sap lines, watching hockey on the black-and-white set in his workshop in the basement. I told myself a story about what he had seen in the fire department for twenty-five years, the suicides and house fires, the flipped cars and bodies cut out of them. It's a small, safe town but I knew that he had cut down friends from their hanging rope. I knew that he had found kids who had tried to hide from the smoke in their closets, and a woman pierced through by a steering column, crumbled against a tree on a dark road. In the story that I tell myself he drank because of these memories, to relax, to make his long, retired days sweet as they should be. But those bottles haunt me, the piles of blue or brown glass that they hauled out for the recycling truck, that one public admission of guilt. I was surprised he didn't drive down to the recycling center once a week to keep his addiction private.

When he was a kid, Robert collected his father's empty bottles. He had rows of them in his room, set up against the window like the back of a bar. Vodka and rum, whiskey, different shaped beer bottles, brown and green and clear. The light through all the glasses turned color on the rug, like light through a stained glass window. We sat in that light; let it fall over our laps like bright, calico cats. I remember holding a beam of blue from a vodka bottle, the blue on my skin, bright and incredibly beautiful. Robert loved the bottles. I wonder if he kept them out of embarrassment, if he didn't want them going into the recycling bin at the end of the road where all the neighbors could see. Or if there was something else in them that he loved, if the spirit of what had filled them called to him like sirens begging men to drown in dark water. Robert picked up drinking early. Our childhood friendship had fallen away, when he was thirteen and I was fourteen.

Robert started stealing beers and then sips of vodka. He would come to class drunk, or get drunk at lunch. He listened to punk rock and wore Doc Martins that laced up to his knees. He bleached his blond hair white. He crudely sewed patches from bands onto his jacket and backpack. He started smoking cigarettes. I have this very clear memory of him leaning against the four-sided monument outside of our high school. One side for the Civil War, one for each World War, another for Vietnam, all the local causalities listed on those broad, smooth faces. I remember seeing him leaning against one of them, waiting for the school bus, and smoking. He couldn't have been more than fourteen, with his high boots and leather jacket and spiked white hair. The last letter that I had written him told him that I wasn't in love with him anymore, and I didn't want to be his girlfriend. I had sent it from summer camp. I blame myself; I think, maybe had I not kissed another boy, had I stayed true through those six weeks apart at summer camp then maybe he would look like the boy I remembered, tanned from sailing, in clean, bright cotton with worn boat shoes and his grandfather's boating knife in his back pocket.

Then, while I was away at boarding school, Robert started going through his family's medicine cabinets. My mother told me over the phone that I should send him a letter. I thought about it. I had written a short story in class about the two of us fishing for brook trout in the stream that ran through the low part in his family's pasture. It was good, and it was mostly about him. I thought about sending him the story, or a note just to say hi, but I didn't and his addictions got worse. He stole his grandparent's pain medication. He started buying up other kids' prescriptions when they had their wisdom teeth removed. He stole cash from his parents' wallets and bought a few pills and then whole bottles. He crushed them up and snorted them. He bought every drug that was for sale in our little town. He drove down south and bought other things, drugs we didn't have in our high school. He started using needles and melting the drugs down and injecting them into his arm, into his neck, into where he thought his heart was. That's what people said in town. We never spoke about it.

This was years ago, in the time between our relationships. We didn't meet up again until our early twenties. I think about that open space often, it follows me down to the Cape, this nagging place of regret; I wonder if his family can see it. In the island house his father is surprised to see me in the kitchen, he feels badly about being caught in the liquor cabinet. He gets another tumbler from the cupboard and offers to make me a drink. I don't like to drink when I am with Robert, because he says that even the taste of booze on my lips is hard for him. He can tell, even if I brush my teeth. But I know he'll be out late fishing on the pier. When the darkness comes to him, he's gone with it for hours. His father tells me that he's going to make the house drink, he calls it *The Cape Special*, and it's three shots of rum over ice. That's it. We raise our glasses to each other without saying a toast. I take my drink upstairs; I say good night to the ladies playing cards, and to his sister and his cousin who are lying on their stomachs in their bed watching Gilmore Girls on DVD, their blonde hair touching at the ends of their ponytails.

I leave the tumbler sweating on the night stand. In the kid's bathroom with fish on the tiles and a lighthouse shower curtain I take down my hair, brush my teeth, take my pills, and wash my face. I pick up my rum and climb into my top bunk, holding the glass over my head like it's a torch. The night air comes through the opened windows. I leave the little bedside lamp on, for when Robert comes back in. The night air moves the curtains. I can hear the pines shaking their small branches. I can hear the surf pounding on the beach and the women downstairs talking low and the girls watching their show together, like sisters. It's very lonely, the sounds of a family that will never be mine no matter how I want them to be, the sounds of an island in the middle of a cold dark bay, surrounded by the beautiful lights of strangers' summer homes. I suck on the ice cubes and let the rum numb the edges of the world, like the rounding off of sea glass.

I look down at the hand-hooked rug, with its gray and blue and white fabric ropes twisting into each other. It's worn by boys' feet and bleached by sunlight. I look at the print of the cloud giant marching through the huge pink and blue thunderheads above the children with ribbons and the ruffles on their summer dresses. I am alone with a ghost of the kid that I knew so well.

Robert, forever a little boy, wild in the woods, in the pinewoods of home, in the barnyard and the small brook, walking between the cows, finding the secret places in the forests that we named like we were mapping the world. He was the first boy I kissed; our hands sticky with pine sap. We climbed above the canopy and looked down over the tops of the trees to the river and then slow danced to a song on the radio in my bedroom, solemn and kind, mixing our tongues, opening our mouths to each other.

In between our friendships, on some summer night like this one, with the dark wind and the trees breaking and everyone busy with cards, Robert took a fistful of pills out of his bag. Maybe with the blade of his pocketknife he cut them into a fine dust on the blue dresser. Maybe he rolled up a piece of paper and snorted the whole pile of powder and was thrown backward onto the rug by the force of the drugs. He lay down in the center of the hand-hooked rug, in the swirling center of the whirlpool of white and blue fibers, like it was an island in the center of the ocean. He floated backward into the darkest part of his brain, one step at a time. He moved from sleep to where dreams live, to a coma, his body becoming still, his heart beating jagged, then that fist of a muscle relaxing, flat-lining. White foam formed on his lips like the sea foam that the Little Mermaid became when she died. He lay there, on the island of the rug, his arms and legs spread, floating between death and something else. By the time his brother found him, Robert was dead.

Maybe his father worked his heart back to life, so hard he broke three ribs. Some one told me this, I think. Or maybe his father just sat with him in the ambulance on the ride down the causeway to the hospital in Hyannis Port where Robert dug himself out of the coma, one dark stone at a time, until his gray eyes opened in a room one night, full of flowers, his father asleep by his side. He was fifteen then, and it would take two runs through a twenty-eight-day program and a year studying in India, praying, bathing in holy waters, walking holy mountains, fasting and being blessed by men in bright robes, before he was even half-alive again. He sweated himself inside out, gave up meat, dairy, sugar, quit smoking, devoted himself to yoga and meditation. After that his gray eyes were always ancient; they were the eyes of an old man

Looking down onto the rug I picture him laying there, in this house that is so much nicer than the house I imagined. I'm disappointed then angry with myself for being bitter. It makes it worse that it's so beautiful, so rich, and so perfect. It makes it worse that it is so comfortable. I picture his small body, his Peter Pan body, stunted on that threshold, forever young and fighting age. I picture him floating there, drowning, and passing through the shadows in his head. I didn't know him then; it's hard for me to even imagine his face. I didn't see him until many years later, at his brother's graduation party, all lean and empty in the cheeks, recovering from another trip to India.

We don't talk about that time in his life or the space between our relationships. We don't talk about the hospital, rehab, or India. The only scar that remains is a dark tattoo on his left arm, a screaming skull surrounded by lightning bolts, the logo of some punk band that he had idolized during that time. It had healed poorly so that the ink looks crackled, like weathered stone. I trace the skull, the lightning bolts with my fingers. I try to heal it.

He wrote me love letters from that little room when he was a boy. He described the Fourth of July fireworks, fishing and sailing and the lobster boil on the beach. He sent them to my home address in New Hampshire, to my camp address in Maine; he drew on the envelopes, little boating scenes, and sunsets over Hyannis Port. I picture him sitting cross-legged like an Indian on the bottom bunk, using the Boy Scout manual as a desk, writing bold love proclamations to me, happy in Neverland, the boy who marveled at the light through the glass bottles, who created a cathedral out his father's secret.

I think that if I could go back in time and help him on the night he overdosed that we could be whole. I envision going back to save him. Sometimes as myself at that age, my sixteen-year-old self, bold and terrifying, unaware of my own beauty and rage. This sixteen-year-old, with her own heavy burdens, holding him that night, standing and rocking him on the rug. But mostly I see myself saving him as an older woman, as a mother, as myself fully grown, filled in around the edges. I go to him in a nightgown, woken from sleep by his pacing. I sense his unnamed grief, his feeling of being burned alive. I steady his hand. I take the pills and shake my head, and he's ashamed, but I won't let him feel that. I hold his head to my breast; he's shorter, younger, so I hold him there, and I take him in my arms and rock him like a child, swaying back and forth. We sit on the bed together, and he cries into the cotton of my nightgown.

I imagine he settles himself out on my lap, until the tears become sleep and I tuck him into bed, laying his blond head on the pillow, and I kiss him between his eyebrows and leave him resting, loving the man that he'll become, loving the little boy who had been my friend. I want to make things better for him, to save him from parts of himself that he never lets me into, or speaks about, but which I can see, like the dark mouths of caves at the back of his eyes. I want to have been there to help him so that I wouldn't have to lose him again and again. I want to keep him for myself.

Robert's ghost lies there, under the picture of children and their big, imagined world where giants walk the earth. I remember the kingdoms we built in the barn, in the fields, in the basement of our homes, the bright cathedral lights on the floor in his bedroom. I picture his drowning body, the foam at his lips, his arms reaching out.

On the pier Robert casts his line out into the black water of the Cape. Across the bay the lights of Hyannis Port shimmer and break on the waves. The wind tears the tops off the swells. His hook catches on rocks and seaweed. He throws the line into the wind with great, gentle sweeps. I imagine him there as I fall asleep, alone, a figure on the rocky pier, his form against the lights of town and the dark, cool water. In the night he comes back into the house. His family has left the lights on for him. I've left the light on for him. We all want him, so badly to come home. His eyes are gray as the storm clouds. I imagine them shuttering to sleep under his thick lashes, beaten by salt wind. He goes to bed without saying anything to me and as he turns the light off that little, drowning boy on the rug becomes dead white in the moonlight. I lie still, waiting to become the woman who can save that child.

Dear Billy the Kid

1.

THERE IS SNOW, JUST ENOUGH to fill the creases in the tin roofs and the rocks in the hills, not enough to even the ground, only to accent its eccentricities, to show its great flaws. Everything is closed, except a gas station where drug addicts watch CNN above the register, and a state trooper stalks the aisles, waiting for one of them to fuck up. Main Street is dark but I drive it anyway, just for a look. I read somewhere that a flash flood dug a river through here once and that all the back doors became front doors because the street was one long channel, a drop off, a canyon. I can't see it but I believe that its there.

2.

We are past the point of convincing ourselves that this is love. Which is a relief to some extent, like letting someone know your real name. It was nice having something noble to fight for but at least this is honest, as honest as we need it to be. I have been listening to songs about you since we came to this state. Bob Dylan says it was freedom they wanted to take from you, freedom that Pat Garrett was hired to steal back and lock up. Beethoven is buried in an anonymous pauper's grave. Your gravesite is cluttered with plastic roses, faded around the edges by the sun, and people visit it, touch it, rub the luck from the stone, stand by the wrought iron rail and watch the shadows spin out over the desert. Does your ghost believe, with the false hope of history that you were something more than what was hunted, shot down and thrown in the ground?

3.

We love our failures. We study them. For years historians thought you shot left handed because of one old tin type where you hold a rifle, prone, to your flank, until someone noted that those old photos were mirror images, flipped on the plate. But they wanted you to shoot left handed, blindfolded with the longest odds because that would have made you more special, instead of a poor, city kid who learned to steal and kill instead of read and write. In the night you shot blind into bushes, pulled men from their horses, matched blood with blood. On the run I think you couldn't sleep, I think you dreamt nightmares all about you. In the movies you lay out on the desert floor like a sunbather, listening to the coyotes call and the campfire snap, watching the great wheels of stars shift above the mesas. We think of that as freedom. But sleepless you watched the sky for morning, you listened to the brush for footsteps, for the snap of pistols, to the sound of horses moving up the draw.

The Real Estate

I DIDN'T NOTICE THE HOUSE the first time I drove by it, I was looking for the address of the apartment I was renting. Everything I owned was stuffed in my car or strapped on the roof rack. A storm had blown through town and left the roads slick and black and the hills so white that the houses stood out rudely from their shoulders and flanks. My landlady's directions took me up a road that slipped through a slim hollow split by a brook, all bound in ice solid as Gothic cathedrals, and then up a sharp hill to the left, into the quiet of the pine forest. The driveway veered off where the road became a one-way track of clay and soil sunken over hundreds of years, bordered by high snow banks.

I set up my books, my mattress, I unpacked my clothing, I filled my fridge, and I watched night come to the field. I didn't check the weather in Cairo, to see if it would be cloudy or hot as Robert walked to class. I didn't open the books in which he had written his name. In the new place I thought about tomorrow, or five years down the road, and he wasn't there waiting for me with his thick hands around a cup of tea. Our separation seemed final. Never had I had such dreams of independence, like Isis without Dylan. With my life unpacked I sat before the window as it framed the twilight.

I saw the house through the bare trees, white and luminescent in the reflective light of snow, a thin exhalation of smoke rising from its square chimney. It stood out, glowing celestial as the storm clouds cleared and the dome of the heavens sat cold on top of the world.

In those poor dark days of late winter I walked the sunken roads and learned all of the houses. The family at the bottom of the road had a yellow lab named Seamus who would follow me until he was called home, but the dogs that lived next door had an electric fence buried around the perimeter of the yard so they would follow me silently, like zoo animals. My landlords I knew well, their golden retrievers, their two sleek Audis, and polite greetings.

But the old white house that I could see from my window had no routine, none of the messiness of human living, no tracks to the door or catalogs in the mailbox, no trash on the roadside of lights as the day dimmed. The address was 44 Flint Hill. Even saying that now, I shiver; it's like an evocation.

—

I couldn't stop looking in on the house. It wasn't like spying, in fact I felt like the house was pleased by my attention. I'd wave at it as I drove by and smile if I jogged past. It feels good to be something worth looking at. The house had not crumbled, had not fallen into disrepair, it was aware of its true angles and good pine floors and how the bubbles in the old glass windowpanes where like freckles on a blond face in midsummer. It lay in the sun of spring like a great cat with the light golden on its strong lines and crisp clapboard. Finding that house empty was an insult. Forty-four Flint Hill was noble, informed by the geometry of ancient democracies and the hope of the first settlers in the great pine wilderness. These weren't values that you just walked away from. It was an empty box, waiting to be filled.

Forty-four Flint Hill's story came to me in bits and pieces, like a quilt made of scrap material. I put it together and wrapped it around my body. The house was more than a building, with walls and a roof and rooms and floors. It had a past, like a family, a story that was beautiful and sad, retreating back into myth. The buildings were handmade, not some factory-generated piece stapled together like the home that I grew up in. My best friend lived in a home built from the same blueprint as my own, copied all over the neighborhoods. There wasn't another place like 44 Flint Hill; it had been built from its surroundings, sitting comfortably on the footprint of the front lot. Its pine boards came from the last big pines, boards four feet wide and straight as pillars. Its foundation stones and front steps were cut from local quarries, dragged by horses up from the ledges and cliffs, all granite, the glittering bone structure of that country, ancient magma ground by glaciers.

The house had values, like a person. It was simple but elegant, like a lady who knew the importance of clean lines. It was just a little bigger than it needed to be but not bold in its size. Its windows were positioned for beauty and light and also for symmetry. All of these things were balanced, function, design and construction. Its shape, its elegant boxes, had the dimensions of old world temples. Life and death occurred within its walls, and the dead didn't go far, they slept nearby in a piece of rocky land that wasn't good for tilling.

◂

The Flint family built it in 1794. Captain Moses Flint, a decorated Revolutionary militia man and his wife, Elisabeth, moved from Townsend, Massachusetts, to Lyme, New Hampshire. They purchased land on a hillside that had been logged and stumped. From the house site, they could look down the small valley Grant Brook cut from the Goose Pond watershed to the Connecticut River and the flat intervals of farmland in Thetford and Fairlee, Vermont.

Moses built a house that was comprised of two boxes; one facing the west and the other sitting squarely to the east, connected centrally like the arms of a cross. Each had a fireplace, a hearth in the kitchen and a stove in the main room that heated the bedrooms above it. The windows were shuttered against the hard storms of winter, protecting the expensive hand-blown glass panes that sparkled with small, imperfect bubbles like you see in Baltic amber. A barn sat to the west side of the house and ran towards the road. He built an enclosed passageway between the house and barn for access in bad weather. Another outbuilding rested to the east. Stone walls defined the property's borders, built up over time to keep in a herd of gray sheep. Each season he and his sons stacked the stones higher as the earth was tilled. Most of the trees on his acres had been cut and shipped down river to the mills, but oaks still grew along the stone walls. Spared from the ax they cast deep poles of shade in high summer. Apples were planted in the sloping back yard, semi-wild, bitter American varieties which they ground into hard cider.

Elizabeth gave birth to eight sons and four daughters in the home, some of whose little graves are marked with blank stones in the cemetery a thousand feet down the road. Moses died in 1848, and the house, barns, and property went to his sixth son, George, who spent his life tilling that ground, pruning the apples, building up the stonewalls, and tending to the outbuilding and wood lots. The acres passed to George's son, Moses, and then to Moses's son, Walter Moses. In 1957, when Walter Moses Flint died, the house was sold. The Flint family was scattered throughout the town, but no one wanted the old homestead on the hill. Over the centuries the trees had grown up, hiding the view down to the river. In the winter, the Dartmouth Ski Ways' lift lights brightened the valley.

The little dirt road had grown wider and seemed to sweep up to the front door. The apples were great gnarled wildlings, the barn slumped, the woods were choked with underbrush and berries, the fields had long since grown from garden to hayfield then back to meadow again.

The white home at the top of the hill was sold, after many years sitting empty, as a vacation home. The new owners visited in high summer, when the heat wavered off the white clapboards. Grant Brook ran cool and slow through its granite banks, and little brown trout slept in the shade of the great stone basins below the bridge to Flint Hill. A family from Michigan raised two sons there on the big lawn, one summer at a time. On picnic blankets and bicycles the boys grew each year. They spent those months hitting at the blackberry bushes with sticks in boredom and watching the night come up from the forest and catching fireflies in the long dusk and smashing them into their arms and faces so that they too glowed, or trapping the insects in canning jars and lighting their bedrooms with that pulsing, sensual flickering.

In the winter, spring, and fall, the house sat by itself, holding its ghosts close. An old man down the road looked in on it from time to time. He received a check each month in the mail for walking the property, keeping the propane tanks full, and checking that the water wasn't frozen in the copper pipes even during the coldest of cold snaps. He plowed the driveway a few times in winter and he mowed the lawn in spring and fall. The ghosts looked out through the bubbles in the hand-blown glass windows, through the slats of the black shutters.

Something strange happens to a home when it sits empty. It begins to live on its own, no longer needing human heartbeats and rhythm. It was in absence that the house on 44 Flint Hill grew through the last part of the twentieth century. Spirits of hands and feet crossed the broad pine floors, the counters, and the stairs. The oil and dust of humans became the only human presence, and this thing touched and moved like the Flints once had. The vacationing family could feel this when they opened the door for the first time in the summer. The quick silence felt like they were interrupting something. The house was never empty; it made noises and seemed full of light. Not a haunting, just old and organic growth. It was the family, not the ghosts who brought sorrow into the home.

The husband was a professor at Michigan State and had children late. He was very successful, always too busy; the vacation home had been prescribed to him by a doctor for his heart's sake. But he used the quiet of the summer in the Flint house to write textbooks, taking one of the upstairs bedrooms as a study. He was tough with the boys, both were loud, physical children. They were always in trouble; my landlords remembered hearing them being yelled at from across the field.

Then one summer the professor and his wife came for just a few weeks, alone. During the winter their oldest son had died of a drug overdose. His father had refused to attend the funeral, either out of grief or disgust. Their younger son left their house in Michigan and was never heard from again. In their sorrow, and rage, they summered at the perfect white house. They sat on the porch and watched the deer come up out of the forest to nibble in the garden, tearing at the hostas along the shaded part of the stone wall. The professor wrote his textbooks. His wife walked along the walls and tall oaks. She walked the dirt roads and the path along Grant Brook where her boys had swum and fished. She watched the clouds go by.

The next summer no one came to visit the house on Flint Hill. The driveway drew soft waiting for tires. The kitchen expected the clatter of pots and pans and dinner plates. The beds wanted the weight of bodies; the floor boards the slipping of feet. In those long days the ghosts got bolder; they held back the curtains and looked outside to the barn as it fell in on its frames, gray and ancient. They watched the deer eat all the apples that fall and the lilacs that had been planted hundreds of years before bloom and faded into brown without a face pressing into their sensational petals. They watched the snowfall, and the town plows scrape against the stone wall that bordered the road. They noted the few times the caretaker did a careless job shoveling the drive, working quickly in the biting cold.

That winter, after the long, sad summer, the professor died of a heart attack in his study. His wife found him in the morning, as she often did, but he didn't wake to her touch. That year she lost her children and her husband. In her grief, she joined a Benedictine order of nuns, at a convent in New Jersey. All of her worldly possessions passed to the Church, including the deed to the white house at the top of the hill in Lyme, New Hampshire.

—

I dug up the listing in the town's tax report. A convent with a New Jersey address owned the whole thirty acres, the barn and the big, white house. They had a website; I looked it over. The sisters were devoted to the arts and housed a famous pottery factory on the grounds. In the summers, they taught children how to throw pots on the wheel. The sisters look like women who work at banks or town offices. They are all slightly overweight and plain, with kind eyes, and lips that offered to help.

The nuns used the house on Flint Hill as a place of silent retreat. They came up a few times a year. They were, I imagined, very much like the ghosts, walking silent paths through the home. I saw a car in the driveway only twice, a small sedan with New Jersey plates, but I never saw the sisters. They came and went in darkness. All the rest of the time, on all those other days of the years, of the suns rising and setting, the old care taker made sure it didn't fall down, burn up, or freeze. He couldn't walk well anymore so he never went inside.

—

The summer after I moved to my new apartment I grew bolder. First, I crossed the field and forded the small brook that separated my landlord's property from 44 Flint Hill. I came up through the woods into the backyard that stretched from the porch to Grant Brook, an open ten acres of brush and brambles that had once been farmed by Moses and his descendants. I walked the property line, down along the walls and up to the shed, looking in through the spreading boards and out through the other side. I made an inventory of its contents: sap buckets, an old tractor, stacks of wood and tires, fly rods, snowshoes, and skis, huge-toothed pull saws. There were animal paths around and under it but no human trails. I stood on my tiptoes and peeked into lower windows facing the ski way. The house was mostly empty. The floorboards were broad and sloped towards the union of the two structures, meeting at an angle like swells meeting at the shoreline. It was clean, but just barely maintained. I opened the mailbox. There was nothing there but the neat hexagons of last year's wasp nests.

Then at dusk, one quiet weekday I walked up the driveway like I was coming home. I came up the broad granite steps to the front door. I stood there and touched the brass handle. It was locked but warm to the touch from the sun. There was an older door, where the barn once stood against the home. It was weatherized and taped shut, but the old wrought iron latch opened. I didn't force it. I let it fall back on itself, afraid to peel off the plastic sheeting. After trying the front of the house, I went around to the back and stood on the porch and looked out over the field. There was a view across that small valley through which the sun rose each day and set, leaving long trails of light through the pines and heavy, rounded shadows cast from the hills. From the porch, I peered into the kitchen open around a large island of butcher block. One washed coffee cup sat upside down by the porcelain sink. A staircase at the end of the room led upwards, each stair dipped gracefully inward like the bow of a cello, worn by generations of walkers. I could almost see their heels stepping into the shadows upstairs.

Even as the trees grew leaves and hid the white home from my apartment window, I imagined it, like a cloud bank just beyond view. At night, after work, I cooked simple meals for myself that lasted for days as leftovers. I drank cheap wine from the Country Store in town. My body longed to be touched. I was so alone that I had moments of pure clarity.

But at night, in my sleep, Robert came back to me. I dreamt of him nearly every night that summer. Sometimes the dreams were almost physical, and I would wake up shivering with lust and hatred. Sometimes the dreams were tragic and I would wake weeping, weeping to be free of his ghost and wondering if I could love anything again without his memory rising. I started praying that I wouldn't dream of Robert. At first just under my breath and then I would kneel by my mattress on the floor and clasp my hands together like a child and recite my prayer to whoever listened to these things. I wanted to dream about myself, about my new life. I lay in bed and rehearsed these dreams so that they might stick and I might find myself walking through them in sleep. I held these thoughts in my hands and breathed into them, praying that they would grow and outshine the things that came to me at night.

During daydreams I saw myself in the white house on Flint Hill. Between those walls I imagined myself perfected. My hair was longer and fell in thick natural waves, my face was bright and fresh, always well rested. In the summer, there were freckles on the bridge of my nose. I was a bit taller and my breasts a bit larger. The house had done these things to me, or maybe I had the ability to change all along and was waiting to practice my magic. I wore comfortable old jeans and cotton sweaters. My eyes were the eyes of a watcher, a keeper of the silent, unnoticed graces. I saw the fawning of the white-tails, the spinning of the eagles above the ski way, and the steady path of the honeybees to the apple blossoms. I knew the shape of the snowflakes before they fell. I rolled out crusts on the butcher block and made warm, spiced pies from my apples. I drank tea in the great room near the open fireplace in winter. I read all the books that I had meant always to read.

In the mornings at 44 Flint Hill, I woke to sunlight like the first run of maple syrup. It filled the upper rooms, elevating the dust particles. It was the sort of light that transforms in fairy stories, turns a peasant girl into a princess, a frog into a prince, a pumpkin into a grand carriage. And it blessed me daily. I greeted the eastern sky over the hill and slipped on my boots to walk down the granite steps to get the newspaper. I rested. I felt my strength down to the smallest toe; it connected me like a root to each step I took. These became my daydreams. Myself in that house. My future in that house. It felt right. The house stood there unloved, and I had such affection for it, more than affection, I had the thing that would bring it back to life, the kiss that would raise it from a death-like sleep.

—

I began writing letters to the nuns in New Jersey offering, at first, to take over the role of caregiver from the old man down the street. Then I began to inquire if they were interested in a rent-to-own contract, I said I would happily leave for a few days when the sisters needed the place for their retreats. I printed these letters on nice paper. I signed them gracefully and I slipped them into lovely thick envelopes. I chose pretty stamps and mailed them at the post office in town, handing them over preciously.

I began to make bigger plans for the property, plans that I thought I was perfectly qualified to execute as a farmer and a poet. I had always wanted a small farm. I would till up the great back-yard and return the house to its original use as a homestead. I would tap the maples on the property and make small batches of maple syrup. I would plant blueberries across the road near the little cemetery and tend them until they were old enough to pick. I would cut my firewood. I would clean the barn and raise laying hens. I would get a few cows and pigs each year, raise them for neighbors and then have them butchered in the fall. I would learn to can and fill the shallow granite basement with shining glass jars of beets, berries, and beans.

At the library I checked out books on blueberries and egg birds, taking notes carefully as I read. I walked the property and sketched out plans for gardens and improvements, I budgeted and researched, I told the nunnery about my plans in my following letters, I wanted them to know my vision. They would see the righ-teousness in it; they would appreciate my values and understand the story line. I wasn't going to remodel and rebuild and upgrade like someone else might, turning the home into a luxury retreat. I was going to restore the house on Flint Hill and run the grounds like a homestead, just as Moses Flint and George and George Moses had.

＿

Through the beauty of summer, I waited for a response. I sent a letter each week, well printed and addressed. I felt myself growing into the woman I had wanted to be, but I'd think *if only, if only I could get this one thing, this house, this home.* We needed each other. It was a relationship; we made each a little better. The house was everything to me; I nursed my love every night as I lay down and dreamed the dreams I wished for.

That fall came late. September was hot, and it wasn't until mid-October that the leaves began to fall, bright and dry. I was imagining myself gathering apples in the backward, fixing up the chicken coop for winter, harvesting the last of the garden. I was bringing in wood and baking pies in the early darkness and starting the first, fragrant fires. My dream-self was busy. When I received a text message on my birthday from Robert, recently back from abroad and wondering if I'd see him, I thought I was over him; the house was all I needed. I agreed to meet him for lunch.

Over the table, I found him arrogant and boring, and I had no interest in his travel stories. I was bothered by how busy his hands were on the string of his tea bag. Robert asked if he could see my new puppy, a black lab mix that I had gotten myself as a birthday present and I, in my dream world, drove him up the hill. I told myself I didn't love him anymore. I loved the house. I watched him look at the road, and I saw the stone walls and low banks through his gray eyes, and the bright flash of 44 Flint Hill, and I knew I had made a mistake. I watched my love and realized that this was all for him, these things, the walls and apples and hand blown glass windows. The house was the place I had wanted with him, all those years ago when we were together. It was our dream, not mine.

It was a quiet, hot afternoon. We walked my puppy down the road and sat in the backyard of the house on Flint Hill. I felt welcome there, not like a trespasser, not on the long grass in the pasture. My love for the house was washed away and replaced with him. It came up over me like warm air rising. Robert had been there all this time. I saw his ghost behind mine. I saw his boots by the door of the white house. I saw his hands on the handle of the ax by the woodpile. I saw his books stacked, his backpack hung on the hook. His cup of tea was resting next to mine in the sink. The house had been my chance to love him again, he would and find me there and want the things I had collected, the barn, the stone wall, the view to the ski way, and I would open myself and share this world with him.

I couldn't say a word. How do you say *house* and mean *love?* I wanted to tell him the language of pine boards, old glass, stone, older, purer than affection.

I spent fall and winter trying to build our love a new structure. We saw each other on weekends. I drove down to the south of the state to see him in his tiny apartment near the college he was attending. We ate hamburgers and took long drives in the early darkness. But mostly I was alone, that had not changed, even as the love had passed from the house to Robert again. The leaves fell, and house rose at the edge of the field, like a moon pulling again to my gravity. There was no response to my letters from the nuns. I stopped writing them every week. Sometimes it would be a month before I sent a new one. They became shorter, more to the point. I didn't check the mailbox daily. Instead my words filled phone calls and text messages, long emails to Robert about our futures, about how I thought of him always and saw him in everything beautiful.

But I still pictured myself in 44 Flint Hill that winter. I put on my hat and scarf and went out to shovel the driveway. I dug a neat path up to the front step and scraped the snow off the porch. On the back porch, icicles reached from the eves like bars over the windows. I imagined myself there in the early night, building the fires up big so that the place was full of the bone warming heat of burning wood. I stripped down to a T-shirt, sweating over the stove in the kitchen, stirring a big pot of soup full of herbs I had dried from the garden and root vegetables from the cellar. Robert was in the other room, reading textbooks by the fire. I heard the snowfall on the roof, in my sleep, in my dream within dreams. I woke to touch him. Mice walked the walls; deer picked the last apples from the high branches of the trees. I watched cold sunrises across the little valley with my hands wrapped around a cup of tea. But I didn't spend all of my time there. Days past when I didn't see myself there in the old white house.

I could feel my reserves of hope drying up, like cellar shelves at the end of a long winter. I could see the bottom, the place where I stopped dreaming, where all I had left with was dirt, the shape of my two hands, their heart lines, their short nails, holding onto things that had already passed through my fingers. Out of the bottom of that well came darker things. These things came to me like the shapes that stood just out of my headlight's reach on a midnight road, shapes that I caught in passing, just legs, tall night walkers, eaters of the sky, things that couldn't be caught in dream catchers. They shook their old heads and laughed, pulling back their teeth from their gums. They pretended to pity my faith. They wanted to get closer to smell my hair, hungry and sly.

—

By the spring, I felt ashamed when I drove by the white house at 44 Flint Hill. The road became a sheet of mud that grabbed tires and slid cars off into the trees. I drove slowly, carefully, the shame strung out. Robert and I were crumbling again between phone calls that took days to be returned, and I was learning to guard myself, preparing for a break. He had hurt me this way before, how many times I could barely remember. I could see the end of it. I was learning that spring to keep parts of myself back. I had loved him with such honesty that I had gone all in, joyfully, putting everything on the table. I was ashamed of that, like I was ashamed about wanting the house, seeing it as mine.

Forty-four Flint Hill bloomed that season, an early, explosive warmth. Lilacs filled the air with their heavy purple scent, their blossoms vibrating with the first slow bees, and the lawns flushed green. The house seemed whiter with the snow pulling back from its northern walls. I don't remember the day that I stopped seeing my ghost-self living there. It happened so slowly. I put my head down. I walked by it as I walked by trees and cars. It became a box, an empty place.

—

When I moved away from Flint Hill, I didn't say goodbye to the house. I thought about the place for a long time, but I couldn't visit it. I drove by the bottom of the hill but couldn't take the turn. I don't know what I feared more, that it would have been burnt or restored or just as I left it, solid in history, quivering with its own, pale potential.

I drove up to see 44 Flint Hill last summer. The house was still there, untouched. It was an early night, and there were no lights on. I could see the night sky through the windows, looking through the form of the house. The apple trees in the backyard, the pine tree scratching against the siding, the lilac bushes along the road, the barn in slow collapse. It was just as I remembered it. I looked for ghosts in the windows but it was too dark to see.

The Flood

IT WAS A HARD WINTER. Everything became further away and darker. The roads battered cars; they buckled and heaved and slowed everything down to the point that I stopped wanting to go out. Every time I got in the car, I imagined my own death. I asked myself, *is where I was going worth sliding off the road into the cold water, into a dark tree, into another frozen, creeping vehicle, into the smooth blade of the state plow?* So I cut back. I worked from home. I did my grocery shopping once a week, on Sunday afternoon, although by the time I left the store it was already getting dark around the edges of the mountains and I had to follow the lights of my high beams up the valley road. Other things were cut away, visiting friends, going to dinner in the bigger town, seeing a movie, shopping, going to the gym, all these were nonessentials. I imagined that winter was like the start of the end of days, all of the good things, the extras of civilization falling off.

I saw death everywhere. People were freezing in their homes, the news channel reminded us to check on elderly people, our oil bill asked for a donation to help those who had no money for heat. People got thinner, tougher, and meaner. I didn't make eye contact in town. I pulled my coat collar up and my hat down over my eyebrows. I kept safe at home.

Joe and I started to lock the doors when we were out. I don't know if we ever spoke about it, or if it was just something we both felt at the same time. We locked up the poor, little cabin, and all of our poor, broken things inside of it. People were stealing dogs and selling them. People were taking the copper and gold out of the underbellies of cars. They were even carrying off firewood. We watched the long driveway for strange headlights in the dark and looked in the snow for tracks, for footprints, for signs.

The cabin we were renting sat at the base of a cliff, covered with tall, straight spruce trees. There was a swift stream that ran between the cliff and the house, always in white water, stumbling over huge boulders. The stream rattled and spilled down through the rocks, collecting in big pools, bottomed with smoothed bedrock or soft sand. Just below the house the stream flattened onto a broad flood plain, mingling with another mountain brook. The two waters came together and raced along, white towards the Connecticut.

The cabin was heated by a cast-iron woodstove. There was a backup propane heater in the living room and another in the bathroom downstairs, but we could never figure out how to run them because the instructions were in French and the pilot light would not stay lit, it would flicker blue and then vanish back to air. The stove ate through wood; it burned fast and hot. The place had been a summer home, and looking to make money quick, our landlords had done almost nothing to winterize it. There were gaps under the doors, and where the windows met the wall. There was a hole in the ceiling above our bed through which wasps spilled in the summer and in the winter the cold would come in and hover over us as we tried to pull the blankets up. Worst of all, the house was built on stilts because the stream flooded often. They had surrounded the stilts with black plastic and fencing but still the cabin sat on air, a freezing pillow of winter that reached up through the floor. The dogs would refuse to get off the couch; the cats would walk the backs of chairs, over lamps, across the windowsills to avoid having to touch it. The stove fought the cold but the heat wouldn't stick, it would just slip away so that even as the stove-pipe glowed amber, the cold sat in the bathrooms and the laundry room and the downstairs bedroom. The cold was more comfortable in that home than the heat.

That winter I lived heavily, wrapped in layers. I wore two pairs of socks and walked the floors in slippers. During the day Joe and I rationed wood. The winter was so long and cold that we were worried that it might not end and we would be left with no fuel. We'd keep the house right above freezing, so cold that the olive oil became solid in the pantry. I lost all sense of my body. I was never naked except for the brief moments between the shower and my towel. I felt like I gained twenty pounds but I don't know, it could have just been that my body became alien to me, strange, a buried thing.

I stayed inside and watched TV wrapped in a fleece blanket on the couch. I cross-stitched Christmas stockings for Joe and me and for each pet. I went to bed early and slept late, following the long darkness. I walked the dogs with a headlight. The trees rose like bodies, the shadows behind the trees became monsters and thieves. The winter made us animals. It took away everything nice and human. We were cut back down to size by it; we were bodies that needed calories and warmth. We could have slept for days, like skunks and bears. We stopped dreaming for anything besides this life. We became smaller that winter, and less beautiful. I lost things I never got back from that cold.

The brook between the cabin and the cliffs had been frozen for months. Early in December I could see running water between the icy banks, but then I could only hear it, dark and rough. The ice grew and grew in the cold of those days. It was the only thing that got bigger. It grew like continental plates. It changed color. Sometimes it was clear, others it was white, or gray. When there was enough sun, it was blue. The blue ice looked like a blade, the blue ice was the ice of the freezing days, when the sun appeared but had no heat, just light in which to cast the world in shadow.

When I was out in daylight, I walked the dogs along the ice banks. It was so thick that it made no sound to walk upon; it was rock or the soil. Underneath I could hear the water, rumbling. The dogs were afraid of crossing the ice in the center of the brook, where they could hear the water. The ice made sounds of its own. It groaned. It creaked and snapped, brittle pops and long breaks. It shuddered like a fallen tree settling into the earth. There were other sounds that were harder to describe, hums, wavering tunes like Tibetan chants that sat right between two notes and seemed to be trying to break the world at its weak parts. Sounds rang along it, down the cracks, through the broad, flat shelves. Dripping and grinding.

That winter the animals became restless. Fox and deer and coyotes stood in the yard and locked eyes with me through the windows without fear. The cats scratched at all the furniture. On the warmest days, I would try to let them outside, but they refused to step into the deep snow. Instead they tore away the legs of our couch. They peed secretly on the love seat in the back room. They shredded it too, turning the canvas into threads. The dogs pulled apart my books. They got onto the couch and attacked the cushions until there were no cushions left; they had all been emptied of their stuffing and flipped inside out.

By the time the dogs completely destroyed that couch, it was early spring. The light was a little longer in the morning and the evening. The sun had some force behind it. I could turn my face to it and feel something in the sky. There was a day of rain, cold, steady rain that beat the snow down. That night we dragged the couch and the love seat outside to the backyard, tired of living with those tattered things, tired of flat pillows and torn fabric. We had to pour gasoline on them to start the fire. We waited until it was dark. The gas burst and then snaked inside the forms of the furniture, under the skirts and up the backs, twisting along the wood inside it, slow at first then smoking. Smoking horrible, thick black smoke that joined the dark sky. It burnt up the smell of that winter, the animals' fur and our skin cells, our hair.

Joe and I stood back and watched it. The light from the house stretched out to meet us like an apology. We didn't touch, we gave each other space like the one, or the both of us might burst into flame too. The snow melted out to our feet. The flames came through from the inside of the furniture, wearing the fabric thin and then bursting out hungrily into the air. We watched it in silence. The fire ate up everything and then gnawing on the bones, the wood, the springs, the bolts, shuddering and collapsing, like skeletons in a mass grave, all the parts mixed up. We kicked the pieces that fell out towards us back into the fire. We watched the sparks rise into the black smoke pillar, following the raindrops back up. Shivering wet through all our coats and boots and hats we walked back up the hill to the bright house. The fire lay in coals behind us, gnawing on the hardest bits.

The ceremony of it all stayed heavy between us. That winter had been hard. Joe had picked up smoking again, standing on the porch just an arm's length from the door as if it might be warmer near the house. When he had quit I thought we might be moving somewhere good together. With each night he shuffled in the cold, sucking on those menthols, I didn't know, maybe we weren't going anywhere I at because I was slipping too. I started seeing things at the edge of light, in the shadows. My fear of driving at night was a real fear. I saw things, my death, the death of dogs, my sisters, huge dark primal monsters made of the hills and spruce and rock. I was scared of little things, headlights in the night, I had to understand every sound I heard, place it, or I rocked myself to sleep, trying to rationalize my terror. The ritual of burning the furniture felt like our first attempt at ridding ourselves of those things, casting the devil out. The house was emptied. We sat at the dining table, looking at where the couch used to be. It reminded me of when we had first moved in, all the blank spaces, and how tender we had been with each other.

In the morning, the fire was still smoking. I took the dogs down to look at it, the bent nails and twisted springs, the feet and rollers and joints of metal all blackened. I kicked some half-burned pieces into the coals. The snow was melted, and the grass was brown around the fire pit. The morning was warm; there were invisible walls of heat in the woods and along the driveway. The sun was rising, laying a thick haze over the cold water. It was the sort of day when you are excited for no reason. I went out to lunch; I didn't eat what I had packed for myself. I bought a twenty-dollar bottle of wine for dinner.

Coming home, the ice along the road was still solid. I could hear the water under it from the car, running, running. At the cabin, the ice was still solid on the brook, but the water was so loud, a contained scream down the valley. The rain had loosened the sand on the hill, and snowmelt ran off it, picking up big stones and dropping them on the ice like canon balls. The stones would bounce off the ice, bounce into a tree, they rattled down with the water or punched their way through. The water ran like a trapped thing. I couldn't hear myself think over the noise. The dogs were spooked when I took them out, the rocks had been crashing all afternoon, the water screaming, they had spent the day looking out the windows, wondering what was happening, wondering if the world was coming to an end.

The rain came again as the night settled, warm and dark in

the valley. Joe and I talked about floods. Two years ago a tropical storm had burst through these mountain streams and cut off towns for days. It took weeks to get past mudslides, washed out bridges, roads swept away. The brook we lived on had flooded; the water had risen under the house and run through the driveway. Huge rocks had bowled down the hill, knocking over trees in the front yard. Gravel and riverbed were strewn through the woods. The driveway disappeared. A big section of the hill had fallen into the river. It remained a crescent of naked sand and rock where a few trees hung. It was an ugly slash on the hillside right across from the porch; we had looked at it all summer. We also drove past a safe and a refrigerator that the flood had swept up into the trees along the driveway, mixed with river-bottom and debris. The people who had been living there when it happened had been stranded; the water pushed their cars up against the pines. They had walked out over the field to the higher, paved road when it was safe to leave the house.

We talked about the cuts on the trees along the river that had been made by the flood, how high the water had been, how strong, that it would use stone and wood to cut through things like trees, riverbank, to cut away forest. All the time the noises outside got bigger. The rocks were breaking open trees on the slopes, popping, crashing, and punching through the thick ice and the hiss, the scream of the water. The dogs were looking around in terror at the noises.

We lay upstairs and listened to the ringing, crunching, punching break up. It was like a storm but not from above. It surrounded us. At some point, deep in the night, there was a strange, big sound that woke me from sleep. The dogs were sitting at the window; the puppy's head was cocked to the side. I was too afraid to go to the window and see what they were seeing. The noise settled and the night lay broad and uninterrupted after that, sleep flattened my fear.

At dawn, we could see that the ice had broken up in the night. It was piled in tall cairns in the front yard and it pushed against the trees along the driveway. The water ran open, seething, twisted gray and white water, so loud as to need to be yelled over, it hissed and boiled like static. With the dogs I walked around the piles of ice, some pieces were a foot thick and stacked in piles six or seven feet tall. These heaps bordered the river; I had to climb to look down into the flood. Some of the ice was cut into bricks, and other pieces had been moved in huge, flat sheets, like counter tops, and plowed through the yard, to the distant pines. Our fire pit had been washed clean, erased, only the grass kept its char. I found pieces of the couch springs in the driveway and charcoal that had been pushed hundreds of feet away by the water.

Sometime in the night, the water had jumped out of its banks and knocked the ice back into the trees. The stream had used our driveway as a riverbed until it found its way back to the low ground by our mailbox. For some time in the night, we lived above a huge, rolling lake of ice and snow melt, a flood, flashing through the land around us.

I found a brook trout resting on top of a stack of ice pieces like it had been placed there carefully. I took a picture of it with my phone. This beautiful, bright fish, recently dead and still colorful, six or seven inches long, ended up on top of the ice which had been its ceiling for months. I thought of its strange death, the fear of the flood, the shattering of the ice, the change of its world, gasping for air in the cold night under the dark sky, raised up like an offering to the low clouds. It wasn't transformation, the slow dawn I hoped for. The thought of the flood roaming our yard in the night scared me more than the endless cold of winter. I imagined water running under our home, under our bed, breaking through the trees, the flood erasing our coals, as if nothing we did mattered and no one would remember.

From the Blue

THE FIRST DARK CLOUDS MOUNTED the hill to the west, flowing over the gap to the north and south so that briefly the farm was in a pocket protected from the rain and wind. Then the storm moved over the hill and filled the sky. I drove down to the strawberry fields as the thunder started and I called everyone out of the fields. The kids on the farm crew collected the quarts they had picked. I told them to wait out the storm at the cabin by the river. Out of the rain, they sat on top of the picnic table on the porch swinging their tanned legs and telling the same inside jokes that made them laugh every time. Before the sun rose that day they'd started picking strawberries. I brought them breakfast sandwiches from the café down the road, and we'd all eaten together, sitting in the straw aisles, as the sun broke up the mist from above the river and the field started to quiver with heat. They had worked on the farm since they were just twelve or thirteen and now, turning eighteen, the girls were easily beautiful, while the boys still looked like children.

Many of them had known each other since birth and it was their last summer together before college, the sense of leaving made those mornings in the strawberry fields, with the shimmering heat and the sun burning their backs, more meaningful. I had worked picking strawberries when I was their age and I knew how much it hurt and how much you could love the people you worked with, how much a sunrise in the strawberry fields felt like your whole body was changing, and so was everyone else's, like magic swans turning back into people. Sitting on the picnic table, leg to leg, they were happy the storm had interrupted the day, pleased to be going home early to swim, or to sleep off their sunburns. I left them there and took the quarts of berries up to the farm stand.

The storm surrounded the farm. I carried the berries into the stand and ran across the road to close the sides of the tomato greenhouses. In the rain and wind, with lightning snapping, I swung the bars around like a sailor, lowering the plastic sides. I latched the back, and front doors closed. Soaked, with my clothing tight to my skin I went back to work in the greenhouse, letting the storm blow itself out. The sun came out to the west as a new set of dark clouds rose over the hill and closed into the north. It would be a stormy afternoon, waves of green on the weather radar like banks of breaking waves.

My boyfriend, Joe, came over during his lunch break to tell me that he'd heard from a friend's Fire Department radio that someone had been hit by lightning at a farm about two miles to the west of us. The Fire Department had gone over there, but it sounded like the person was dead at the scene. It was big news in a little town on a Saturday in June. He told Maddy and Max as they passed by putting away their lunches. We stopped to talk, wondering who it might be, how it must feel to be those farmers. It was scary, and it changed the way we looked at the clouds.

I drove down to the cabin and brought the kids back to their cars, just to be safe. We shut down quickly that day, closed the barn doors and finished the work in the greenhouse. Big storms rolled through all afternoon, one after the other, then a brief opening of sun and blue sky. The whole day was ruined, broken up by weather. When I got back to my house, there was a message blinking on the machine. Max called; he had heard from a friend that the person who had been hit was Caleb Baker, the brother of one of the girls who worked at our farm, one of the girls who had been down in our fields picking that morning. He had heard, too, that the boy wasn't dead, that someone had gotten his heart beating at the scene, and he was in the hospital now. I had never heard Max's voice so serious and it hit me somewhere deep in the pit of my stomach.

Caleb's sister Lucy was the leader of the group of kids who worked at the farm. She told them which swimming hole they were going to visit after work, when they were allowed to take water breaks, who was a bad picker and who was doing a good job. It came naturally to her. She was tough, with bright hazel eyes and the wild Celtic curls. She had slapped the first boy who tried to kiss her. Her mother was delicate and quiet, while her father was huge and kind, with a big truck. He was the sort of man who lifts you off your feet when you hug him. I had met Caleb only once, years ago, when he was still a little kid. He had the same eyes as Lucy, and the same thick eyebrows.

That evening, as more storms rolled in, Joe and I got dressed up for his grandfather's memorial service. He had died on his garage floor with his head in the lap of his wife of sixty-two years. Joe had been working at the time and called up to the house by the Fire Department. He had almost passed out seeing the body there, of this man who had been more a father to him than a grandfather, this man who had taught him to fish and hunt, and turn sap into maple syrup. He had also shown him how to check out women and gamble. Joe wore his grandfather's golden gambling ring, this huge gaudy thing, whenever he got dressed up to go out. I had noticed it on our first date; it had been the most interesting thing we talked about that night.

His body had been cremated and put into several small jars. One lived forever in the rafters of the sugar house that he built with Joe, another in the corner of the milking parlor on the dairy farm he and his brothers had run. The largest jar had spent three seasons on the mantel above the woodstove in his old home, where his wife was getting sick of looking at it. She had kept all of his things, his guns, boots, his cars and work gloves, but she felt like it was time for him to pass along. Relatives from all over the state had been called up to gather this day, and they were going to go through with the ceremony, no matter the weather.

We took the interstate down to his grandmother's house. There were two deer dead on the side of the road. No sign of death, no blood or guts, it was just like they had dropped into sleep. They lay right across from each other, facing opposite directions. It was hard not to see that as a sign. Did someone move them into that position? Had they been struck by one of the day's lightning bolts and in their final terror split up, one running to the left and the other to the right, before life left their bodies? I once had a dream that the road was filled with dead white-tailed deer and the only way to get where I needed to go was by driving over their soft forms. I thought about that dream and the two deer in their strange death. The clouds were pink then and dark purple, as the storm lit them from behind.

Joe's family trickled through his grandmother's little house, eating cheese and crackers, drinking sweating beers and glasses of white wine with ice. People talked about the kid who had been hit by lightening at the farm; the information was repeated over and over. He had been struck, but his heart had been started again. He was in the hospital. *The Bakers were good people; Dan Baker was a fine carpenter, a strong man, he was a good softball pitcher, it was too bad.* I didn't want to say that I knew Lucy. I disliked the way the stories rolled around like glass marbles in people's mouths, turning color and growing larger.

Solemnly the family, friends, and spouses walked up through the woods with a storm rising again over the hill to the west. The forest was wet, and the trail turned to mud. A girl who had been dressed for a party complained, she hadn't thought the service would be held on a farm. The dead man's children led the group; they were already crying as they walked up through the property. His oldest son, Richard, who everyone called Rick, held the small jar in both his hands like it was too heavy for just one. We came out at the top of the pasture above the dairy farm. There was a view there from under a wild cherry tree, down the valley, and across the river into the hills of New Hampshire. The whole farm spread out like a map, the road cutting its green fields in half, the barns and outbuildings distant and clean. Above the farm the sky boiled pink and purple with clouds that rolled over each, letting off shots of bright electricity that made the shadows blue in places. Thunder shivered and crashed, like pots and pans, or hungry stomachs.

Under the wild cherry tree, someone dug a small hole. The jar was put in there and covered with casino chips. A couple of people gave brief speeches, talking into the vast, terrible sky. Joe was crying, gasping for air. I held his arm like he might fall over. I had never met the man who was being laid finally to rest, so I just absorbed the grief of those who grieved, felt sorrow for sorrow's sake, and thought about death in general, not just the death of this one man.

The storm followed us back home and sat above us all night, clawing at the window, lighting the night so that sleep, despite the wine, came in quick flashes, a patchwork of nightmares followed by startling darkness. I woke up knowing that it would be a rough day. I showered and brushed my teeth and put on my best face.

At the farm a mother of one of the kids was waiting for me, pacing behind the barn, her arms resting on the small of her back like it was sore. She wanted to see me in person; she hadn't felt like more phone calls. She told me Caleb was in the hospital, deep in a coma. He had been struck directly by lightning and his heart had been stopped for minutes. One of the women who worked there had been to nursing school, and she beat on his chest until his heart started pounding again. It didn't look good. She wouldn't tell me that he wasn't going to make it; she didn't want to be the one who said those words first, but I knew. Lucy wouldn't be into work that day, neither would Anna or Emily who had known Caleb since childhood and who were all now by his side, watching him in the darkness.

I told the other kids this as they gathered in the barn for our morning crew meeting. They were solemn, eyes downcast, drained of their sunlight and laughter. And two days later I told them that Caleb had died. I gathered them all around. I wore sunglasses because I was worried that I would begin to cry. I told them that he had been in a coma and passed away early in the day.

It was true, but not the whole story. Caleb had been struck directly in the head by a huge bolt of lightning, a bolt from the blue. It traveled out ahead of the storm, reaching down to the ground hungrily. His face and chest were burned, marking the entrance and exit of that electricity. He had dropped immediately, so quickly that the boys who were hoeing next to him didn't know he was missing until they saw his body quivering on the soil. Kristy, the girl who worked at their farm stand and was also a nurse, had given him CPR for five minutes before the ambulance arrived and had gotten his heart to start before he was rushed to the hospital. The doctors knew immediately that he wasn't going to make it. He was too far into that blackness; his brain was dead to any future of life, swelling and filling with blood. His family had called all of his friends to his bedside to say goodbye. For two days they flowed in and out of the children's hospital. The nurses set up space in a conference room with food and drinks for all the kids who came to see Caleb. Some of them slept there, in the waiting room, folded in little chairs like cats. The space filled with cards, balloons and flowers. The crazy woman who lived down the road from the Bakers came and said that she could feel that he was gone. She was physic. She left them a crystal and a bouquet of wildflowers.

Early in the morning, when all his friends were asleep, and the hospital room was empty, his family had the nurses take him off life support. They stood by him and watched him move finally into death. First, they checked off the long list of organs they approved of donating. Lucy told me later that the one thing she told them they couldn't harvest were his eyes. She was scared of running into someone, sometime down the road, who had her brother's eyes, which were so much like hers that it would have been like looking into a mirror and seeing this stranger with Caleb's eyes stuck in their head.

After I told them about Caleb's death the crew was silent for days. They bore their sorrow, their fear, even guilt, with good manners and grace, holding back smiles intentionally, casting their eyes toward the soil. I spent the days researching lightning and policies that would prevent something like Caleb's death from happening at our farm because there were too many *what ifs?* to answer. I learned that he had been working with a group of his friends. They had been called in from the field by radio, but the communication had failed, broken up by the storm. They had been trying to finish the row they were working on when Caleb was hit. The lightning jumped to several other boys, too, who were hurt. Shocked, they had hidden under a pickup truck at the edge of the field, watching Caleb's body shake and then go still, too terrified to move, or even call for help.

One day, only a few mornings after Caleb's body had been removed from the hospital and buried in their family's plot, Anna and Emily showed up at the farm to work. They didn't call; they were just waiting, with the other kids, standing in a semicircle around the white board where we gathered. In our morning meeting, I welcomed them back. I told them that they had been missed. With their heads bowed, they slid back into line with their friends, leg to leg, arm to arm, happy to be busy, to have things to fill a day besides hospital chairs and cafeteria food. I thought that they might have been changed, aged, or in some way been harmed, so I tended to them. I walked around the edges of their lives, carefully, ready to catch them if they fell.

Lucy appeared a few days later, her face set against any sign of emotion. She was thankful, she said for everyone's support. She told me she was sick of staying home and eating desserts. All they had in the fridge was dessert, cakes, pies, cupcakes, cookies and brownies. Lucy said that she wanted to get out of the house. Her mother cried all day. Her father was busy arranging things, thanking people, shaking their hands when they came by with more cupcakes, and setting up the memorial service. She worked through the morning, shoulder to shoulder, all the kids weeding at the same pace like they couldn't stand to leave anyone out. I drove by them in the truck, and they were silent. They didn't look happy, or sad.

Two weeks after Caleb's death his family organized a memorial service. They held it in the high school gym. The day before they asked the community to pick flowers from roadsides and gardens. They said they wanted real flowers, not the sort that you can get in grocery stores, so that the stage would look like a walk through town, with everyone's gardens on display, the bright sunflowers and white Queen Anne's lace, showy perennials and loose wild rocket.

Lucy wanted to pick from the gardens at the farm. After, I offered to teach her about flower arranging, something the crew didn't get to do. We gathered scissors and knives, filled plastic buckets with water and walked across the road to the rows of flowers, rippling in the breeze. We talked about what sort of flowers Caleb would have wanted. She thought he would like the rudbeckia, cultivated varieties of black-eyed Susan, because they looked both like wildflowers and shooting targets, and cleome, because the leaves looked like marijuana and he had started a few plants in the woods that summer. She planned on growing them out and smoking the pot in the winter, as part of some ceremony celebrating his life. We cut and stripped the stems of cleome and rudbeckia, and let the cool water soak up into the stems. We picked and picked until the buckets were full.

I asked her if she missed him. She said that she didn't feel like he was gone. It was silent in their house, she had noticed the absence of his voice, but she still felt like he was away at camp or visiting a friend and could come home in a few days. His room was very messy, and she didn't know who would clean it up or when and what would happen with all of his stuff. She had taken a few things out of his room, his iPod, his pot pipe, his journals, things that she didn't want her mother finding and that she felt she should have. She had been putting together a play list for his memorial service and wanted to use songs from his iTunes account. It took her a night to figure out the password. Finally, after hundreds of combinations, she discovered that it was CalebRocks. She thought this was stupid and funny at the same time. She didn't know when she should start using the past tense to talk about him. She didn't know why people wanted to see her cry. She said she cried a lot, she went up to their tree house and cried for hours, but no one saw her. All of her friends cried, all the time, and she felt like she was disappointing them.

Before the memorial service, the farm crew changed out of their field clothes. We let anyone who was working take the afternoon off to attend. Almost everyone came. The gym was packed; it felt like the whole town had showed up. People were standing in the aisle and along the back wall. Caleb's friends, teachers, and father spoke at a podium under the basketball net. They projected funny pictures of him on a huge screen and Lucy played *Forever Young* on her guitar. The stage was crowded with people's flowers, like their gardens, like a walk through town. The rudbeckia and cleome that I had picked with Lucy sat in the center of the display. Afterward, I stood in a long line, eating cupcakes and drinking lemonade out of paper cups, waiting to shake hands and to hug Lucy and her mother. Her dad almost picked me up off my feet, turning our handshake into a hug.

When there was a storm later that summer, we quit working immediately. Everyone went inside at the first clap of thunder, even if the sky was blue. I made Lucy call her mother to tell her she was safe. Instead of working in the fields I made long lists of fact on my laptop, learning everything I could about lightening. I learned that cloud-to-ground lightning bolts are a common phenomenon—about one hundred strike Earth's surface every single second. Each bolt contains up to one billion volts of electricity. Some types of lightning never touch the ground but travel between differently charged areas within the clouds. About two thousand people are killed worldwide by lightning each year. Ninety percent of those struck by lightening survive. They suffer from a variety of lasting symptoms, including memory loss, dizziness, weakness, and numbness. Most of those who are killed by lightening are male. A *positive giant* is a lightening strike that hits the ground up to twenty miles away from a storm. Because it appears to strike from a clear sky, it is called *a bolt from the blue*. These bolts from the blue carry several times the destructive energy of other lightening strikes and are the most deadly. Thunder can only be heard twelve miles away under perfect conditions so these bolts can find you even if you can't hear thunder. Lightening can also occur during dust storms, forest fires, tornadoes, volcanic eruptions, and even in blizzards. The science of lightening is called fulminology, and the fear of lightening is astraphobia. Lightening oxidizes nitrogen in the air into nitrates, which are deposited by rain and fertilize plant growth, fixing nitrogen in the soil. The French phrase for love at first site translates literally to a lightening strike. Zeus, Thor, and Indra were lightening gods, and Christ's second coming is promised to be lit by lightening, huge sheets of it brighter than the sun. Lightening is caused by the sky rubbing against the earth, ice separating from water and becoming positively and negatively charged. Water on water, air on air. If you have been struck by lightening and survive, you have a greater chance of being struck by lightening again. These things became a shield, they rationalized and calmed. They allowed me to make plans that I thought could protect people I loved. I don't believe in luck, or fate. I couldn't make sense of Caleb's death any other way.

I have always been a storm watcher. I loved to fall to sleep to the crackle of lightening and the roar of thunder. It wakes me, full of fear at the world, and its pure, huge forces. Lucy told me that she regrets that her brother's death changed the way she saw thunderstorms, they make her sad now when they once made her excited. I admit that they scare me a little more. I watch them coming and think of the water around us. It is hard not to look at the clouds and think of the oceans of on top of us. We live on this little island of land, surrounded by waterways, the rivers, the lakes, and oceans, the streams below us, the aquifers. Bodies break and return to water and carbon. We all run out, eventually to the sea or rise up into the clouds.

The Man in the Ground

A THOUSAND YEARS AGO IN the hills of Korea the hunters fasted and remained chaste. The plant they were searching for was said to have resembled a fallen star in the forest, which only the pure could see. Looking over the hills in the night the plants flashed in the hollows and narrow wooded canyons and in the shade of northern slopes, in the huge ancient woodlots. When one of the hunters saw the forest light up an archer would shoot an arrow to the spot, marking it so that in the day, when the plant's brilliance had faded from the bright sky, the hunters had only to find the arrow's painted shaft. But they had to be careful; there were bandits in the wilderness, thieves waiting on the roads and path to steal their harvests. Tigers prowled. The banks were steep, the rivers wild and white.

The root itself was guarded by a demon, which they believed would lead men further and further into the wilderness, to their death. They hoped their purity would protect them; they would pray to the root they sought, to the tigers, to the spirit of the mountain. Like all hunters I expect that they also believed in luck. During the days that I searched for the root, I was never hungrier, or more aware of the holes in my life. We were all looking for a plant that made promises.

Ginseng is described in Chinese medicine as "the essence of

the earth in the form of a man." It was a king's herb. In 1596, the Chinese doctor Li Yenwen wrote, "the cool nature of fresh ginseng expresses the yang influence of spring, of Genesis, of development, the yang of heaven . . . and the yin influences of the earth." The root contained all things, heaven and earth, man and the gods of the wild. The medicine itself took the shape of a man, a root split and splintered, gnarled, twisted in the form of arms and legs. Over the centuries, Imperial hunters stripped it from the forests of Korea and Manchuria.

Ginseng is a sensitive plant. It requires deep shade, on northern and eastern slopes and prefers sweeter soils, growing near oak and birch, maple, rarely around pine and spruce. It thrives where the boulders tumble down mountains, in the steep places men avoid. When I hunted it, I learned its habitat; I stalked it down the hills into the heart of the forest. It develops slowly, a root the size of a thumb takes five years to grow, living underground, even the cold heart of winter. In late summer, an orb of red berries rises from its central growing point, a flag for hunters and an invitation to birds and beasts. I've been told that animals recognize the strength of the herb and use it like medicine. Rutting stags eat the berries for stamina and the birds swallow them before their long flights south. Ginseng seeds are scattered in scat, but if they evade consumption, they roll off and establish large plots, swathes of the ginseng washing down rugged draws, like a river of plants.

I hoped to find the oldest roots, and the twisted ones that were said to be more potent since their price per pound was higher and an ancient or perfectly man-shaped root could be worth thousands of dollars. A ring circled the root for each year it has grown, marking the notch where it has set leaves. They can be counted in centuries, these old roots. But that requires hundreds of seasons, unnoticed, in the high places of the temperate mountains. Five thousands years ago the Vedas listed ginseng as a powerful herb, and it was hunted to the ends of the known world. By the middle of the seventeenth century, it was a ghost, a golden specter in the hills of China and Korea. Its value increased with its scarcity, making it more holy by its evasion, like a mythical creature. Diggers continued to hunt for it, going higher, deeper than their fathers or grandfathers had traveled, bringing the twisted roots to the markets of the great cities and to the doctors of the imperial family, trading gold for gold.

In 1714 a Jesuit priest traveling through China became convinced of the healing powers of ginseng. He published a paper on the root in a British medical journal, which was read by another Jesuit missionary doing God's work in Canada. That missionary, Joseph Lafitau, thought he had seen something similar to the botanical illustration in the forests behind his home in Quebec, the American species of the root, *panax quinquefolius*. Iroquois and Mohawk medicine men told him that they used it to treat headaches, fevers, gunshot wounds and to revive those close to death. Latifau sent roots to the Jesuits in China who confirmed that the plants were nearly the same and could be used interchangeably. Profiteers began using native people as hunters, paying them to search the hills and dig the roots. In 1783, a merchant ship sailed from New York to the Pearl River in China with thirty tons of ginseng, pulled from the forests of Canada, New England, and Appalachia.

The ginseng hunting business spread, local diggers sold to middlemen who hauled huge harvests out to the offices of trading companies in major ports. It became a common way to make money off the wilderness. In his youth Daniel Boone searched for the cluster of red berries, lighting up the shade of late summer in the primal forests of the western hills. Men at the edge of the world combed the shade for its red berries. But ginseng does not grow near men. It is a recluse, tired of civilization, so as if chased, it receded before the folds of settlement, moving ever deeper into the wild lands. Soon, the great shade forests of hardwoods along the spine of the Appalachian Mountains were logged. The outlaws that once hunted it moved west. Farmers settled and the few ginseng roots that survived deforestation were bleached by the sun, or eaten by half-wild hogs and sheep. But in the steep ravines, the ginseng remained, retreating each year into a deeper shade, into the heart of the mountain.

Ginseng harvests came in waves, as old hunters died, their children didn't inherit their treasure maps and protected patches in the forest. To maintain supply, hunters became cultivators, caring for the wild plant, planting the seeds, and digging only the biggest each year to ensure a harvest in future seasons. Some hunters tended their ginseng like farmers, others roamed and stripped, coming in the night with lanterns, digging up a patch that had taken another man his lifetime to maintain. Ginseng hunters walked with rifles and stalked low through the forest. They remembered again those prayers for safety.

By the 1970s the plant was mostly gone from American and Canadian forests. It was declared extinct in some states, rare in others. two hundred years had seen forests regrown, some places had gone wild again, and others had filled with homes and cities. Where I searched for the root, in the soft valley of the Connecticut River, between New Hampshire and Vermont, the hills were once more thick with trees. There was still a vast market for the root in China and money to be made hunting for the plant. In states across the Appalachian Mountain chain, it was declared protected or threatened, so agencies issued licenses, established age requirements for the root, harvest limits, and hunting periods. In some places, it was illegal to be caught with ginseng root, dried or fresh. In others, a slim margin of weeks was set at the end of summer when it could be collected from the forests. I had a permit, stamped by the state, which I carried with me in the pocket of my jeans.

I was a farmer in the valley, and my boyfriend, Joe, was a mechanic. We worked with our hands each day. Debt pressed on us, accounts of student loans and credit cards. We lived paycheck to paycheck and felt like were digging ourselves out of an impossible hole. Hungry for more, we started hunting. Joe's grandfather had harvested ginseng behind his dairy farm, in the old wood lots left to go back to oak and maple. The land there was steeply hilled, cut with cliffs of granite, falling into deep streambeds. He had taken Joe with him when he was a little kid, a treasure hunt in the forest. Walking slowly, they watched the ground for the plant's distinct leaves, and for the bright red berries. They carried a little trowel, to dig out the white, twisted roots slowly, leaving no arm or leg behind in the ground. He showed Joe under which trees it grew. Oak and maple, poplar and birch, in the shade of northern- and eastern-facing slopes or up against the trunks of fallen trees. In the quiet places far from the yard, fields, the old woods, in the places left uncut, unwanted by man.

Joe's grandfather would dry the roots on a window screen in the basement. He would cut them up and add them to hot water, a bitter tea which he claimed would make you stronger, faster, and better with the ladies, he said. Some years, if they found a good patch, he would sell some of it to a friend. This other old man bought up lots of the roots and then drove them down to China Town in Boston where he sold them to an herbalist. It was a yearly trip, going down to the city with a bag of roots and coming back home with cash.

Joe's grandfather had died a year ago, in the summer, just when ginseng plants are red with berries. Joe had held the older man's body, on the floor of their garage. Being witness to this death defined his future; it created a straight line through his life, *before and after.* He visited his grandfather's grave to ask for advice, sitting in the high pasture over the dairy farm and talking to him in the evenings. He remembered all the things he had been taught by the old man, how to turn sap into syrup, how to walk the woods in November hunting white-tail, how to bait a hook for trout, how to fell a tree and dry it and run the splitter, how to spark a fire in the woodstove and run it to heat the house all winter, where to find ginseng growing wild in the forest.

One night, drunk on our porch, watching the white water in the stream, Joe and I decide to go looking for it. In the morning, hungry for money, we climbed the steep hill behind our cabin. We crawled up through the gullies, and waterways cut through the topsoil, and we looked down on our roof, on the tops of our cars, our garden, our porch, and our yard. We hiked toward the old hardwoods and searched around their skirts. The humidity of late August drenched us in sweat. At each fallen log, or rock, or around the base of each old tree, we were filled again with hope. But we found nothing.

The next day we drove to one of the places Joe had hunted the plant with his grandfather as a boy. We parked the truck on the side of the road, and we walked in, through the edge of someone's yard, quietly. We moved just past where they mowed and maintained and down in the wood below a cliff. My nerves made the sounds of the neighborhood grow louder around us, dogs barking, kids playing, cars grinding down gravel driveways. We searched through a strip of forest where the slope was too steep, where the shade was deep and the trees old. It was unwanted, edge land. Boulders the size of cars and bookcases rolled to the base of the hill, and ferns grew between them, in the laps of deep-rooted maples and birches. We walked without compasses, following waterlines and road noise up into that hidden place.

We swept over the ground, high and low, over the rocks and below them near a stream, searching. Looking for red in the green, like a blood trail. We moved slowly, with our hands behind, jumping from rock to rock, peering in the shadows of those stones and along the lines of fallen trees. We didn't speak to each other. We were silent as thieves.

Joe found a patch of ginseng, in full berry, bright above the five spread leaves flowing from a rock wall, down to the stream, like water. He slipped his finger down along the stem of every plant, revealing the neck of the root with its rings of age. The longer the neck, the more it twisted down into the earth, the older the root. The deeper he dug with his finger, the more our excitement grew. He pulled the soil back and counted then began to dig the root itself, creating a broad hole around the plant so that each turn and fork was removed. The root was a white, twisted thing. It looked tortured.

When the ginseng was free, he snapped off the leaves carefully and tossed them aside. He stripped off the small red berries and carefully planted them around the hole, where ginseng had been proven to grow well. We went through the whole patch like that. Digging down to count the rings on the neck. Scooping the dirt away from the oldest roots, prying them out. Planting the berries. Leaving the small young behind, ensuring that next year we could come back to this place and dig more.

The roots smelled bitter, like something you weren't supposed to eat. I put them in a bag I carried over my shoulder. We found a few more plants, dug more roots and put them in the bag. Back at our home, we laid them out to dry on a window screen, in a darkened room upstairs. Each root was different. Some were like men, split four ways from a central trunk, others were like carrots or parsnips, some spun around like funnel clouds. Dirt stained their rings, marking each year the plant had struggled to grow, sprout leaves, and continue in the rock and dark. When he was sick that summer Joe would cut a small piece off a root and soak it in hot water. If we were going out to a party, and he was tired, he would do the same. Sometimes he chewed it during the day when he was out cutting wood, believing in its medicine. In the bitterness. I could never get past the taste.

On the weekends, we hunted the woods around town. We found the places the old men told him about, sharing their secrets since he was the only one who asked. Some days we didn't find a single plant. Other times we found groups, clusters, the berries' brightness lighting up the shade. We never found a patch that would make us rich or a root that was more than twenty years old. We walked and hiked and double-checked the steep valleys and northern slopes then laid the roots out on the window screen and watched them shrink.

In early fall, we found an ad in the classifieds for a ginseng buyer. He paid cash and only used cell phones, like a drug dealer and he appeared at our cabin one night, in a clean black car, with a small scale. He had a Chinese girlfriend whose grandfather had an herbalist store in New York City. He promised the best price through this connection, Chinese to Chinese. He weighed out our roots, counted their age, and noted their splits. The ugliest, oldest ones were worth the most. He zipped our harvest into clean plastic bags and then he did the math for us, the weight multiplied by the price he was paying that day, scribbling the numbers on a slip of paper. He circled the total as if to get our agreement. *Four hundred eighty dollars.* From an envelope, he counted out four crisp new one-hundred-dollar bills and four crisp new twenties. He gave us his business card and asked us to call him again if we found more.

That cash felt good. We split it between us. Two hundred forty dollars to each wallet. Over the next week we spent it, on wine, on weed, on a dinner out in town, on a new dress, on ammo, all of these little things that dogged us daily, those little wants. It wasn't wealth. Ginseng hunting was like the myth of a money plant. It was a lot of work, but the promise was enough to bring us back again the next year.

We widened our search area, going higher, deeper into the woods. Discovering new patches. We took over the secret places of men who were dead or dying. The cash slipped away and I came home bruised and covered in bug bites, with hard chips of mica under my nails and slashes on my shins from blackberry brambles. The places we dreamt of reaching but never got to rose like huge mountain ranges, just past my reach.

My Wrong Love Story

I.

MY COLLEGE BOYFRIEND, JASON, MESSAGES me on Facebook to say that he is getting married. He doesn't know the how to word it. Then he disappears from my friend list as I'm typing, *wishing you all the best.* Someone says he moved to South Africa. There is Robert, the boy of a million second chances. The one whose heart stopped, stilled by the pills he snorted off his childhood bureau at his family's beach house at Cape Cod. I say I won't and then I do. I mail my house key to India. I send him my address in a text that arrives in Cairo, brightening a phone in his back pocket while he's out with another woman, a woman who looks just like me. Sometimes these messages arrive with no response. Sometimes he calls me on my birthday after a year apart or sometimes he sends me a scarf from Thailand. Sometimes he lets himself into my apartment in the middle of the night. He has that key I sent him, the lock slips open in his hands. He can see in the dark like a bird of prey, walking through my same old stuff in this new space, and finds me in bed, drawn by my heartbeat, my body temperature, and my second chance scent. He leaves me before dawn. And the night comes to me again, like a huge dark cat. I think of those people who raise panthers, sleep with them, so comfortable with their big cats until one day they catch their pet looking at them hungrily. The night looks at me hungrily. It isn't my friend anymore. It wants to tear out my stomach. It wants to strangle me with its teeth. It wants to eat my body away casually, over the course of many days. It wants to leave my scalp, all the bloody bits cleaned up, like a dirty mop head on my kitchen floor.

2.

By the time I meet Joe I've stopped believing in love. He is nervous on our first date and he gets drunker than me on tequila shots and I lead him back to his truck. He hugs me and doesn't take more than that. He texts the next morning asking if I want to hang out again. It's easy, and he is handsome. He lives in a trailer, and cooks me Rice-A-Roni for dinner, his hands shaking with nerves. He shows me his baby pictures and pours me cheap wine that sticks to my teeth and lips and turns them dark red. I light up cigarettes inside while we lie on his old, stained couch, wondering how many girls have crumbled in those pillows. I sleep over in his twin bed with camo-fleece blankets. Sometimes Joe doesn't have the money for kerosene, and the heat gives out in the middle of the night. The pipes freeze and buckle, and we wake with our breath above us. He loves the simple things that I wished filled me up like they did when I was younger, like the light in the forest, docks on the river or the distant mooing of cows. We rent a place together miles away from everything. It is hardly a home, more like a tree house. It's January when we move in. I strap my mattress to the roof of my car and drive it north in a snowstorm. The cold is bitter. It is biting. It finds us sleeping on the mattress in the middle of the living room, the fire almost burned out, the floor too cold to touch. There are gaps under the doors and around the windows. There are holes in the wall where I can look out and see the pale dawn. There is trash in the backyard and no cell phone service, but there is a bright sunrise over white pines and a river choked with ice. I tend to the place. I put too much money into it, into its rough parts that cut me, the holes where wasps and mice spill into the bedroom; the gaps where the winter slips in through. The cats and dogs find the sunny spots on the floor. We try to make the best of it. The night there is real night, dark and scary. Joe falls asleep early, stoned. He isn't handsome when he sleeps. Those first nights in the house I cry. I huddle in a corner upstairs. I hold my legs to my chest and tell myself that tomorrow I am going to be happy. The details of our life stack up in my chest, the holes in the walls, the bills, and the dirty floors.

3.

The fact that he does it all right shouldn't frighten me but it's all so strange. First, Joe tries to trick me into thinking we are doing something else but he's not that good at acting and it's the hot end of a long day at work and I know I am being tricked but don't really even care to think about why. He takes me hiking. We never go hiking. He walks in front of me even though I am always in the lead. These things bother me because I am in much better shape than he is, and he is walking really slowly. At the top of the hill, the trees have been cleared from a rock face, and the mountains open up to the north and east. Hawks spin in the clear summer sky. In the valleys, the white steeples of churches mark the centers of little towns. Joe tells me to wait and goes off into the bushes. When he comes back he's shaking with nerves, carrying a picnic basket, his face white and shining. He kneels on the granite. *This is it,* I think, this is the moment I have thought of for so long. I tell myself to enjoy it, to soak in the beauty from all the edges of the world to fill me up with something. But really I am embarrassed for him. And I worry that a family is going to hike up the trail and see us and I'll have to cry and smile and they'll probably take my picture, and I'll look like shit and wish I'd had time to shower and change. We sit down on the rock and drink a glass of champagne together out of champagne flutes that I realize he borrowed from his mother. There's a red rose in the basket too, like in *The Bachelor*. I am shaking. I am terrified. I start to cry, to drizzle; it's like a draining. *I'm happy, I'm happy,* I say. And I am happy to be chosen, to be worth a ring, champagne, and a rose in a picnic basket. But I know I am going to have to tell everyone, and then plan a wedding and then have a wedding, and I begin a week long panic attack, which is just functional and well timed enough that everyone assumes I am shocked and overjoyed. But I feel like I've walked up to a mirror and been surprised to see an entirely different person looking back at me. I take off my makeup; I strip down naked, I scratch my arms and see the woman in the mirror with scratches ripped red down her arms too. I get dressed and follow my mirror-self home to her house, to her bed, to her car and couch and kitchen, and I learn where she keeps her forks and moisturizer and which light switches don't work and the sounds that the train makes in the night because this is now my life.

4.

I make an appointment at a fancy store that has its own reality show, and I invite my mom and Joe's mom to come with me. *It's not about me,* I tell myself. I arrive on time to the clean store in a Persian suburb of Boston, in the bright air, wearing the underwear and shoes that I've read I should be wearing. Everything is wrapped in plastic and impossibly cool to the touch. I run my hands up the skirts of dresses I don't want to try on they are so expensive and so beautiful they'll break my heart. I run my fingers along the beading of gowns as heavy as chain mail, against lace that is scratchy and lace that is soft, gowns that are violently studded with rhinestones and others that are simple as cream. The store is busy that day so I can only try on five dresses. A saleswoman, wearing all black, takes them from me, one after the other. She comes into the curtained room after I have stripped to my nude underwear and strapless bra. She is kind and has seen this before and works like a nurse, slipping the first gown over my head then buttoning it up, telling me that it looks lovely, and I know she says this to everyone, in every dress. I am too small, so the woman in black puts huge clips down my spine to make the dress fit. I walk out to the open room of mirrors. Next to me a young Italian girl is drowning in the puffiest dress I have ever seen. On my left, a blonde slips into the white pillar of a gown, preppy and simple as the columns on Dartmouth's library. I have never been so surrounded by women, mothers and grand-mothers, brides and babies. I am waiting for a moment when the *right* dress will find its way to my body, and I will be so sure of its rightness that I'll burst into tears. I know this won't happen, but I want it to. I look at three angles of myself, standing high above the dressing room floor, on a little podium, wearing a bedroom's worth of fabric, waiting, just waiting for something to feel right. I watch my Mom's eyes, hoping that she'll see it first. I look at the other women, the sales lady, the friends of the Italian girl, the grandmother of the blonde, for help. In the end I compromise on the best of the imperfect, last seasons gowns. The dress I buy is in my budget, it almost fits me, it is a white A-line with a little bit of beading. It has pockets. These are the details that sold it to me, and the way my body looked almost like I imagined in its chilly white satin. The saleswoman slips it back into its cool plastic bag and car-ries it out to me from behind the desk. I want to hold it on the drive back home, press it to myself like a child with its blanket, trying to find that smell, that scent that would make it beloved.

5.

I remember my high school roommate showing me how to walk in heels. She led me across that Michigan campus, walking behind me, checking me out like a man. She was a pretty midwestern girl who was embarrassed to have done some beauty pageants as a kid. She clucked her tongue and told me to walk like a woman, hip to hip, not like a drag queen playing around in heels. Her memory comes back to me while I'm shoe shopping. I know exactly what I want for my wedding shoes. The beautiful thing is that no one is going to see them, my dress is too long and full. Once in a while a toe might peer out like a shy kitten, or a heel may get hooked on the tulle, but they are private shoes. The shoes say, *fuck it*. They are three-inch heels, the sort you could walk in all day but still look dressed to kill. They are made in London out of white silk and hundreds of shining white crystals. They are completely plastered with these gems. I imagine they are like Cinderella's shoes if she was performing in Vegas, a showgirl's glass slipper. They can't help but catch the light and break it a hundred ways, like in a rage they took all the crystal out of the cupboards and threw it on the tiles to make a sun catcher, and they don't regret it. They are shoes sharp as a backhand. There is no justifying them. They are the unexpected guests I am too scared to ask to leave because they might stand up during my ceremony and never hold their peace.

6.

In the bathroom upstairs with the bad overhead lighting and the small mirror, I lean in and I stare at myself. I mark each blemish, each dark spot and line, like I am creating a map. I follow my wrinkles to their base. In pictures I try to find the moment when that face changed, when my smiles stopped being natural and white, when my cheeks were still high and full and my fore-head smooth as clean sheets. There aren't many photos of me from the last few years. I have been hiding from cameras, cell phones and Facebook posts afraid of this version of myself standing with my family and my friends. The cosmetologist promises to help me get my face back. She sells me creams and sprays and masks. She pops every pimple. She suffocates me in warm towels, and herbal steams. I have never felt so dirty, as when I am lying in her clean, white office, smearing towels and stainless steel with the ooze from my face. She electrocutes the worse offenders, the zits that are so deep that they are like toxic waste buried in the deserts of my cheeks. It feels like running your face along the inside of a hot dryer, full of static electricity and prickly, cotton lint. Afterward, I look roasted, like meat. I put on the lotion. I look at myself again, shining like Easter ham. I let the creams and washes and masks become a routine that equates beauty. I rely on them. I have faith. I repeat: pre-wash, wash, toner, moisturizer, day cream, pre-wash, wash, toner, moisturizer, night cream. I come to the mirror in the morning with hope. Please let me see myself beautiful again.

7.

I close my eyes and picture myself as a grown up, I don't feel like one yet. I look at the woman I see there. She is calm and graceful like a dancer or like a woman who takes art photographs and lives on an alpaca farm in the hills in a restored cottage. She has long, easy curls. She is the woman in the Bob Dylan song about the girl from the North Country. She holds a steaming cup of tea to her face, and the steam wraps around her like loving hands. My hair is in between places. It is confused. I wear it in a bun that falls to pieces. I braid it at night, so it doesn't tangle but still in the morning I lose handfuls of it in my brush. I don't wear it down often, like the woman I imagine because it is heavy and hot, or static in the winter, and I am unsure if I should blow-dry it, curl it, or straighten it. I have had short hair and very short hair. I have cut my own hair with children's safety scissors in my dorm room at art school, violently, like some girls cut their wrists or thighs. I have had bangs. I have had perms. I have dyed my hair darker, almost black, and lighter in an attempt to be blonde for one boyfriend who said I would look hotter as a blonde, but it turned out a light, horrible orange. I have donated a thick braid of my hair to cancer wigs. I have never loved my hair, or hated it, or fussed with it too much. I look at that imagined woman; I picture her on her wedding day with her long hair like good silk, and I vow to grow my hair out. I skip appointments at the salon. I tie it up as the weight increases. I think that everything gets stuck there like spiritual glue, all the good and bad, the anxieties and crying fits alone in the bathroom, they grow into and through my hair, into the rings of growth. I read somewhere about ash from ancient volcanoes being found in the rings of old trees, marking their age, dating those eruptions. Poisons, a reading of tragedies, this is the stuff that I can't wash out, I can only cut it off, freeing myself from my own history. But I have vowed to let it grow, to let this stuff build up like toxins. It gets heavier, it starts to smell of darkness, one inch a month, and it creeps down my body. I will wait, I tell myself, until the morning that it curls around my face like a lover's hands, like the girl in the song, and each long piece reads its own scripture in brown-inked cursive.

8.

I take my dress from the closet, my huge pillow of a dress, down to a seamstress in the city. The woman is small and exhausted. She isn't bitter, just business-like, removed from my joy and my fear.

Her little dog follows me around. She tells me she walks it a stroller. She worries about the little creature getting in fights with bigger dogs or picking up dirt on the side of the road. She takes my gown from me, strips it from its plastic and hangs it on a hook. It looks like a mermaid caught in one of those huge trawlers that sweep the ocean. I take off all my clothing while my mother watches and stand, in heels, on a little platform in front of three mirrors. When have I ever been this exposed? My nude undies and nude strapless bra render me Barbie naked, all the parts the same color as the body. The woman, with pins on her wrists, slips the silk over my head. It falls over my body like cool water. The dress fits me loosely; it hangs over my small breasts in two full folds that are so deliberately empty that I feel personally insulted. The woman tucks and pulls, using sharp little pins and huge clips; she works on her knees before me. I raise my arms like a crucified criminal. I stare past and through myself, through my mother, through the woman, taking pins from her mouth, making the dress fit me because I failed to find a dress that fit me. Like finding a man and then changing him to be my perfect man, this dress will only be my dress after it has been cut, pinned, taken in and let out, hemmed to my small height and pressed under steam. I leave it with her to perform her surgeries in the shop with the little dog, hanging again in plastic with a dozen of other women's dresses. I think of the dresses, and it fills me with shame, something that can't be cut out, only worked around, like broad shoulders and tiny breasts.

9.

I like the idea of being masked slightly; it will buy me, I hope, a few seconds of grace to catch myself. The big doors will be open like stage curtains and I'll see my sisters lined up looking at me. Everyone will stand as I step over the threshold onto the rug laid out to the altar. My father will be guiding me. I'll hold onto him like I never have before. I'm worried that I'll smile, or worse laugh, at how strange it is. It's just too personal, I don't want to be seen. I look at veils online, cheap ones and ones that cost more than my car. Veils that make you look like the date of a detective from a black-and-white film and veils that make you looks like a hot nun in a telenovela. They come in floor length, cathedral and chapel lengths, elbow, cheek, waist and waltz length. I drive down to the city after one of my fittings and try on veils in a fancy bridal salon with my mother. We get coffee at Starbucks; she calls it a *girls' day out*. I let my mother crown me with each of these veils, the long ones, the fun short ones, the romantic ones. There is something fantastic about them; they are so far removed from their intent that they are just thin memories, metaphors of metaphors that lost their meaning centuries ago. I move like a princess in a movie I watched too much as a girl. I want to be covered, clothed and left alone. I fold the veil over my face and feel safer, hidden, like my problems aren't mine anymore, like no one can read my eyes. Behind the small nets of lace I could be dreaming about hamburgers, or the dark handsome men I will never meet, while looking down politely, letting my father lead me, remote in my own tower, like the princess that no one rescued, whose hair wasn't long enough to use as a ladder, who liked her voice too much to trade if for split legs, who had no interest in spinning wheels and lived the rest of her life happily in the forest, speaking to birds and making birthday cakes with fairies.

10.

My makeup artist does zombie movie makeup. There are pictures of the undead on her portfolio page. Somehow this gives me hope. I want so badly to be a different-faced person that if she can turn models into skulls whose flesh is rotting back from the hairline, whose lips are just teeth, then maybe she can change me. She asks me at my consultation how much makeup I wear, I tell her, *almost nothing. I dust on some powder. I have the same old slimy tube of mascara from college; that's all the magic I can work.* She sits back and looks at me. *You are such a natural beauty, you probably don't want to wear a lot of makeup at your wedding, otherwise you might not recognize yourself. That's the point,* I say. Leave no scar exposed. Laden and lengthen my lashes. Paint over every crack in my forehead. Leave only the framework of my bones as identifying marks. On the day of the wedding, she arrives early, and we are the only ones in the church. I open the big doors to the road and small ones in the back so that the wind moves through the building. She sits me up high under bright lights. The silence of the little town runs around us like water around a stone, the slow traffic, the kids on their bicycles, circling, flowing around us. I smell her body; I taste her breath. She is intimately close to me for an hour, almost kissing me, almost brushing her eyelashes against my cheek. I keep my eyes closed like a person at prayer. I open them and look high into the ceiling, looking for heaven; I look down toward the sad carpet of the church's meeting hall. The fake lashes pull my eyelids down like rocks in the pockets of a drowning woman. The weight is real and exhausting, I feel tired already. I look at myself in the mirror she has set up for me, looking, looking, side to side. I can see myself but only the structure of myself. I think of those female secret agents who, with a box of hair dye and some sharp scissors go from blonde bombshell to dark killer in a motel bathroom in just one night. I wish I were a snake leaving its skin, shrugging it off, touching leaves and sticks with its new body, reborn.

One evening, after work, big thunderheads gather like fabric, rising against the hills. I shower and get dressed nicely and drive with Joe in his truck to the church where we are going to get married. The pastor guides us into his office, and we sit in front of him like we were visiting the school principal. He has photos of hiking trips with his family, and paintings of mountain views and sunsets. His name is Steve, and he wants to get to know us. He leans back in an office chair like he's getting ready for a long, good story. I sit very straight, with my legs crossed, I tell him that I grew up here, I work across the river, being outside is important to me, as are my dogs, I love words and books. Joe tells him that he works on cars. The pastor needs an oil change, so they talk about prices, Joe's voice changes and I can tell he is relaxed. I resent that he is immediately at ease with this man, that he has taken this easy bait toward friendship. Steve gives us questionnaires to fill out separately and then return to him so he can combine our answers and help us confront our differences before our marriage. The booklets look like state tests in high school, they are all multiple-choice questions with small circles to fill in with number two pencils. I write my name on one and Joe writes his name on the other. Over the course of a few evenings, I fill them out with false honesty. Why would I reveal my secrets to this man in his office chair who wants to talk winter tire prices? His kindness makes me question my lack of faith; his good books and college education make me wonder how he can believe in God and why I can't. Am I missing something? Am I not getting the names right? I bring the booklets back to the church secretary but in the car, before I go in, I sit and read through Joe's answers. The one thing he would change about me, of all of my many problems, all my anxieties, is the way that I dress. This stops me. I realize that I don't dress the part yet. I dress

like a cool twenty-something, not a housewife in the country. I
remember that Joe doesn't like lingerie. He likes lounge wear. He
loves the soft, simple woman who he thinks sleeps under my skin.

12.

The week before the wedding I take an hour off in the afternoon.
We meet in our work clothes, with dirty hands and bags under our
eyes, and we drive over in his truck, which smells like the weed he
thinks he hides from me by smoking it in there. There is a line at
the town clerk's office, so we sit next to each other in chairs along
the wall. I think of all the times that I'll sit next to him like this, in
hospitals and restaurants, at funerals and other people's weddings.
He is handsome, seeing his face in the office reminds me of this.
There are pictures on the wall of the town's past, families in front
of their farmhouses, horses pulling sleds on the ice, Forth of July
parades and Christmas tree lightings, pie baking contests, deer
hunting weigh-ins. I look into those faces; those black-and-white
and hand-colored faces, and search for the sort of discomfort that
is crawling inside of me, burning my heart. The clerk calls us up to
the glass and slips us government papers. She opens the back room
so we can fill it out on the conference table under the fluorescent
lights. I give up all my information, my parents' names and places
of birth, their education level, my address, my education level, and
my birthdate. I help Joe fill his form out; he can't read well, and
the boxes and lines confuse him. I take his pen and I fill in his
information, his families names, his social security number. I try
to remember all of it because I know that I'll have to complete all
the bills and tax forms for the rest of our lives. I pass it to him to
sign. I sign mine, with my maiden name. It occurs to me that I'll
need to change my signature, I haven't even practiced it. I remember writing out my name and the name of my crush in middle

school as if seeing them together would join us. The clerk congratulates us as she stamps the document official and it is there, in that office, that I feel the most for this man, standing in the narrow hallway of historical pictures, in his work clothes. I promise myself that I am going to try very hard to look like those women in the pictures, sitting on their front porches, shelling peas, gazing down over the field with an old dog by my ankles, blessed to have busy hands and a good view. I try to let that become love; it's a little detail that could grow over time, a short story that becomes the line that defines everything. I take his hand and squeeze it hard.

13.

The night before my wedding I lie in bed as far away from Joe's body as possible. He is deeply asleep, and I have said nothing to him all day. The details that have plagued me have been ironed seamless. At this point, there is no turning back. There are too many mechanisms to stop, the reservations, the guests already arrived, the food all made and piled up on plastic platters in friends' and family's fridges, the flowers cut, dresses pressed, money spent. I just want it to be over. Mom asked me that morning if I was really in love. I resented her for waiting until then to ask me. The truth is, on the eve of my wedding, I dream of a wedding I had wanted years ago, a wedding that will not be mine. I walk through it like the event planner just a few minutes before people arrive, when all the details are perfect, and the wind is the only guest. It is on a bluff on a beach on the Cape. The day is slightly overcast, the ocean gray, like wooden shingles on houses along the coast. It is the end of summer, and the grasses are high and yellow, filled with buzzing insects that play their legs like strings. The tables are laid for just a few dozen. Robert and I have said our vows to each other in private; we'll walk together down the grassy aisle, holding hands like we did in middle school. The wind will take my ribbons and my hair; I'll push it out of my face to kiss him in front of our family and those few true friends that have traveled with us through the years. The scale and simplicity of it speak about my charm and grace, how easy it was to assemble, to pull together, each little decision a quick, yes or no. I stand on the bluff, holding my bouquet to my side, looking out over the rows of breakers, the muted sun resting on my shoulder blades like a warm, kind hand. I close my eyes and walk away. This is not my wedding. Tomorrow things will happen as I planned them. The logistics give me comfort. How am I supposed to feel on that night? Is being nervous the same as having anxiety? All along people have told me, *do what you want, it's your day,* and the hollowness of that lie eats at me. If it were truly my day, I would go back in time to the summer when I was ten. I would pack salami sandwiches and read a graphic novel on the birch tree that hung over the brook while my childhood dog, raised from her sandy grave, swam again in the cool brown water there. Hidden in my castle of pine and oak, I remember being so myself then, every dream I would ever have still intact, nothing spent yet, nothing compromised or wasted on other people. I fall asleep there, with that girl, begging her to lie in my arms and melt back into me.

Deconstruction

I.

I start in November. That month of bone, an X-ray of a season. I look in the mirror and see the things that I have swallowed and the things that remain. The nails and scissors and bolts, the places where I am rotting. Muscle and fat are just ghost images. There are fractures and breaks that I have been ignoring but now I can see them cutting across my bones like cracks in plaster.

2.

I look out and backwards over my life like a view into the fields of my youth. I dig deep in my desk and find my nice stationary. I write an apology letter to someone who broke my heart, reaching out back to him. I want to remember the good and the bad. I say, *I'm sorry, we had good times, great times.* I say, *hope you are well,* then I slip it into the mailbox. It is slick with road salt, the metal cold from the snap of frost. The letter crosses states and ocean and arrives in a gray stone town that it is only a fantasy to me, like the setting of a children's book. At some ancient table he opens it, with his square hands that I know like my own. His life lines and love lines that I read when I predicted a future that we'd never have.

3.

I hold my books and weep. I linger at the edge of the cornfield at dusk, wanting to pass. I wait for something to roll out from the hedgerow like low fog and take me. I wait until the night darkens the world. I wait until the stars appear dimly through the heavy clouds. I wait until the cars pass on the road. I wait until the lights come on in the houses across the river and then I imagine the warm, happy families coming home, setting out their groceries, and constructing their lives in better places.

4.

As the winter deepens my body grows hot, like a reaction to the cold. I want more badly to be touched. I walk the dry snow roads. I walk the edge of the field, wanting hands to slip and brush over me. There is snow on the sharp pieces of cut corn stalk. There is snow on the dry grasses on the roadside. The prints of an owl's wing where the mouse tracks end, a life uplifted, snatched from a path of cold, night, moon, hunger. I write his name in my journals. I dream of his body. I write, *I want to flow over him like water.* His name becomes a round stone, sweet with salt, which I hold in my cheek like a cyanide pill. I trace it with my tongue, dreaming of biting down, or forever rolling it on my pallet.

The Lie

IN THE CAMPFIRE LIGHT MY siblings' faces look spooky and old. We lean in close to the fire to keep the bugs away, letting smoke drift over us like holy incense. Our seats are pine logs set in a square around the fire pit, so from my log, I can look to my right, my left and straight ahead into their familiar, deeply-shadowed faces.

Away along the marshy shoreline the loons that we canoed past in the day are now ghostly mourners. I picture their sharp, red eyes spinning back toward us, I remember how the water ran off their feathers.

Above us, the lights of the big rented house glow and throw shadow into the pines. Upstairs I can see my mother pacing in her nightgown, speaking to my father who is reading in bed. My uncle and his boyfriend are in the kitchen, drinking beers, their elbows leaning wearily on the granite bar.

The lake water ripples in the wind's wake. When fire logs fall into each other they crunch and then sparkle upward, red embers darkening between pine and star. One by one we tell each other scary stories.

Although this is only the first day of our reunion in Maine, we already know our family will never be the same. We all sense it though it is as subtle as the transitions of seasons. This will forever be the before-time, and I'm sad to think of how we'll try to reproduce this weekend in coming years until finally we'll be forced to acknowledge that we are in a different place. Mom's cancer is worsening. She'll start chemo in a few months. Despite the odds being overwhelmingly good, the cancer, which is in her blood, seeps out and stains us, mortality's first touch like a cold night late in summer. There's no hiding it. It reminds me of blackberry juice, a dye deep in the seams of our finger whorls.

Around the fire we are knee to knee. My brother, Jake rubs his girlfriend's shoulder in an offhand, stoned way. My sister, Hannah and her boyfriend, CJ, break up little sticks and toss them into the flames, where they crackle and turn to char almost instantly. Elise and her husband, Dave, have their hands knotted together, all mixed-up fingers and knuckles. Her diamond cuts the light too sharply I think. I am the only one alone; I feel outnumbered.

The sounds of the loons and the flames, the lake, and my siblings' voices overlap and suddenly I remember fifteen years ago Elise and I floating naked in a lake full of stars. We'd snuck out of the family camp where we were bunking with cousins we hardly cared to know. I was fifteen, writing secret sonnets in a journal. Elise was thirteen and lean, spotted with freckles like a fawn. We undressed behind a paper birch. In Maine those nights were as warm as the lake water, so that when we waded in from the shore we might have been walking through air. We breast stroked silently to where the bottom fell deep and the water was cold and there we flipped over and floated and lay still. The lake flattened and turned to a mirror around us. I looked over and saw my sister surrounded by stars. Her hair was cut in a bob then, and her face was naked. Her eyes that gazed toward heaven were the same as my eyes that looked at her across the dark lake water; big, brown eyes that could catch something and hold it shimmering. The loons started calling. We said nothing to each other. I wonder if she remembers or if somehow this is just part of a story that I've written about us. I might have made it up by pasting together two nights, or maybe dreamed of her floating like that in summer stars.

Again a loon cackles in the darkness, that noise I recall is called a tremolo, a wavering. My biology teacher compared it to the Joker's broken laugh. The loons we paddled by in the afternoon dove deep into the lake's brown water, down into the water world of drowned men and sunken boats, the bodies of old trees, lost toys and ancient northern pike with their mouths like saw blades. We waited and counted the seconds, then the minutes, until they bobbed up again. Then a loon would toss the water from its back and fix us with its sharp, red eye as it worked a fish down its tight throat. Now they tremolo in the night, laughing at other loons, or at their own wavering echoes.

I am not thinking of lying or of telling lies. I know exactly what story I'll share but I'm last in the reverse birth order we've agreed upon so I hold the story in my mouth and taste its darkness and fear. My blood turns a bit colder and I open my hands to the fire. The light shines through them pink and red.

One by one my siblings share the same story, the story of the ghost in our basement.

My brother and sisters nod at each other in agreement. This is their mutual ghost, they understand its ways, its lurking, its shadowy form. They've seen it multiple times. They can feel it, even just a few days ago when Mom sent them down to the basement to find the big camping cooler and some Tupperware bowls.

I know everything about this ghost because I created him. It's the ghost of old Farmer Pete, whom our street was named after. Pete chose our house at the bottom of Pete's Lane because he had buried all his beloved pets at the site that was now our home's foundation. These pets, a few barn cats and a mutt dog, would haunt by his side, rising darkly from the sandy soil. Pete could be felt most often standing just behind a person in that eclipse of peripheral vision. He was a dark flash as you spun around. Sometimes all you felt of him was the sensation of being watched. He wore a long barn coat and mud boots, a thick beard and some form of felt hat. I remember weaving Pete together in my imagination and then spitting him out for my siblings on some summer day in our basement twenty years ago. The candles I had placed around us flickered ominously. The Ouija board before my crossed legs seemed to radiate with power. I remember my brother and sisters looking at each other in fear and the story generating momentum and how its energy made me almost god-like. How I savored the feeling of a meaningful story even at the expense of their fear. That was the beginning of the lie.

It seemed so harmless; really just a form of make-believe. But my siblings have carried it with them. It is the scariest thing they can think of, this story I created for them, probably out of boredom on a rainy summer afternoon. Perhaps I was old enough then to have known better. It seemed to me just another of my games, my stories, my characters, but it wasn't really, it was a cash out of trust deposited over many faithful years. In our large family I was the little mother, the babysitter, the cook, and housemaid. So the story was a first act of rebellion, a harmless lie that played on love. What have I given them with this lie? Have I cultivated fear?

I'm thinking of all these things at once, stories, trust, the memory of their young faces, the flickering candles, the flickering firelight, fear and the joy of creating with words, but when it's my turn to speak I stutter out something quick. I tell them the story I've been holding onto, the one growing sour in my mouth, about a dark night in Malibu when the Santa Anas were blowing and I couldn't sleep for its howling and the crying of the canyon's coyotes. There is no ghost in my story, just a darkness like a pit into the bottom of the earth that I felt in the parking lot off of Mulholland Drive where I stopped to watch the city lights. I still can't explain it and I certainly couldn't describe it to them now because I'm not thinking of my ghost story anymore, just the ghost I made, just the fear I planted in them. The loons howl; they wail like wolves. They use this call to regain contact with lost partners in the night. Their call quiets us and the fire seems to die.

The windows in the rented house are dark now. I pull myself away from the fireside. Good night. I hear them kick in the fire and clink together the last beers of the evening.

Upstairs in my room I am alone with my lie. It wants to remain that way. I feel that some things are better left where they are; to uproot Farmer Pete might expose me, and I'm not ready for any more exposure this season. I'm guarding myself and my stories closely. I wrap the lie up with the rest of my secrets and pull the quilt up to my throat. I am sleeping in a kid's room with two narrow cots. As the only single person at the reunion the room is my allotment, to sleep with one empty cot staring at me across the moonlit floor. The second bed is a ghost, too, a reminder of my failures. I shouldn't think like this, I know, but I feel small here. There are framed pictures of sailing boy scouts on the walls and stacks of kid's books on the night stand, stained and dog-eared by summers of renters. I lie, staring at the ceiling in the corner of the vast house, feeling my smallness, my aloneness as true as the dimensions of the cot. I think of my siblings wrapped up in their lovers' arms, my parents, my uncle, all resting beside another's body. I think I might drift away, untethered like a forgotten canoe.

On the drive across the mountains to the lake in Maine, I traveled the same route I'd taken on my honeymoon. The greatest lie I ever told were the vows I spoke in a New Hampshire country church a summer ago. They were so much easier to say than the truth of the matter that I felt compromised and empty and why not?

Over the mountains, on the road to our honeymoon, my new husband snored and drooled onto his seat belt. He'd come to bed late in the night, stumbling up the stairs from the after-party in our backyard. I didn't know what he'd been into, booze, drugs, or weed. It had been hard enough getting him into the car. We left two hours later than planned in a steady, stormy rain with thunder rattling the edges of the windshield. As he slept I indulged in listening to a song that I had shared with a previous lover, a man with whom I had often driven that same mountain road. I thought of him and the wedding I had hoped for but would never have and wondered where he was in the world, and if he was broken too. I cried for a few hours, at first secretly, and then with increasing drama hoping to wake my new husband and be comforted or at least questioned, but he slept across the state line and woke wanting lobster rolls a few miles from the coast. It rained every day of our honeymoon.

Those nights I felt like a ghost in the white lingerie I had purchased. After my husband was asleep I rose from our bed and walked the halls of the house we were staying in. I looked out the windows at the quiet streets and wondered if someone might see me and think I was dead.

Lying comes naturally to me. It gets wrapped up in a tumble of other things that I love, like stories and boldness, and has always been getting me into trouble. When I was a girl, I lied about simple things. During nap times when I was sent to rest in my parents' room, I enjoyed taking the drawers out of my father's filing cabinets, removing all of his files, and then sitting in the drawers as if in a small boat and rowing across the light blue carpet. I'd return the files and knock the drawers back into the desk, but my father would find things out of place. I recall being put in time-out for lying about this, and it must have been the last of several such lies, because I was sent to the attic, a cold, dark, unfinished floor at the top of our house. My father told me the story of the boy who cried wolf then dramatically shut the door on me, leaving me in a wedge of light, huddled on the attic stairs, wondering why I had been told about that lying shepherd.

The place smelled of fiberglass insulation, and the few moth-balls my grandmother kept in her family's ancient railroad chests. I imagined all the animals that might be crawling around me in the dark, the mice and red squirrels, the hornets and bats. I kept my eyes on the slice of light and grew bitter to my father and to the story of the boy who cried wolf. The story didn't fit anyway, I thought. It was about false alarms, saying something was happening when it wasn't. Plus there was danger in the wolf, it could eat boys and sheep while my lie about sitting in the desk drawers had just been a flat lie, and harmless at that.

As a child, my imagination was so vivid that now I can still remember the details of my created worlds. For several years I was very sick and often lay in bed with asthma, reading and being read to so that my greatest friends were characters in books. One summer my only companion was Aragon from *The Lord of the Rings* trilogy. He would wait for me at the edge of the woods as I finished my Cheerios in the morning. I remember the scratch of his bearded face (how would I have known this? My father was always clean shaven.) and the twinkle of his armored shirt in the dappled light of the white pine forest.

My siblings didn't share my imagination, so I set about to make them part of my realities, building elaborate sets, crafting characters, and designing costumes so that our playing resembled amateur theatre. Is it a lie to pretend to be someone you aren't or to tell someone to act differently? I would dye our water with red food coloring so Elise and I could act as if we were drinking wine at our fancy dinner table. I would cast large bones out of plaster and rags and then bury them in our sandy field. The following day, when the sun had dried over my digging, I would bring my brother out with brushes and shovels, and we would spend the afternoon working as paleontologists unearthing ancient beasts.

Of all my tricks and stories it was the lie I told of the ghost that stayed with them. I picture myself at the age of that telling in fifth or sixth grade, aged a bit faster than the other girls, with a full set of braces and a new training bra. I wanted to be part of bigger things.

The ghost of old Farmer Pete grew from my ramblings alone in the woods. Our house had indeed been built on what was once farmland. I knew the dimensions of the original properties from the stonewalls and barbed wire that hung from old trees. I stumbled upon cellar holes and walked the crumbled stone foundations of silos. At the edge of a creek I discovered the farmer's dump and began a careful study of its contents. For a week I trotted out to the site with my mother's rubber dish gloves and a bucket of soapy water into which I sloshed porcelain shards, glass bottles, rusted bed springs and speckled flanks of enamel wear. The bigger pieces, steam tractor engines, bed frames, plows, I dusted off and pulled out of blackberry brambles. Some of the rusty cans still had ancient labels; peas, beer, and powdered milk. I put Pete together from those pieces. I took home a few beautiful cut glass bottles and set them on my windowsill. But I couldn't sleep well with them in my room; they seemed to watch me all night and I felt that ghosts must attach somehow to the things that were once theirs. So I set the bottles in my tree house instead and filled them with wildflower offerings.

Under a great pine tree I found a stash of brown liquor boxes, and digging under the topsoil, dark black ashes. I imagined a man stealing out to the woods to drink in the shade of the tree and, in the winter, to warm himself by a hidden fire. Pete had his secrets too.

At some point our family acquired a Ouija board, perhaps a gift from my grandmother, who claimed to have spoken to JFK several times after his death using the board and its planchette. Elise and I asked it mundane girlish questions like the names of the men we would marry. The board spit back names like Oliver and Frank and we giggled and tried to remember them. We were both lying, of course, both pushing a bit on that little wedge.

The day I created Pete it was stormy and dark and the light hardly fell into the basement from its casement windows. In the summer the basement was the coolest part of the house and we would crowd there, playing inside its cement walls as the house rattled and gurgled above us. Mom might have gone off for some appointment. I was often left in charge of my three siblings for an afternoon. I had set the scene with our long, tapered dining candles, the sort we only took out for fancy Thanksgiving and Christmas feasts. Three of them flickered in the family's silver candelabra. The others were set on the floor in individual holders so that the candlelight created a circle. In the middle of the circle I set the Ouija board.

I guided my siblings downstairs in the dark and sat them inside the candle ring knee to knee. I closed my eyes and told them that I had been sensing a spirit in the basement, and we were going to call to it and bring it out. We held hands and waited until the air grew humid with fear. They placed their little fingers on the planchette, and I asked the basement what was haunting it. We pushed slowly, P.E.T.E., and then all the candles flickered as if a breeze or breath had moved them and we shuddered. *He's here!* I might have whispered.

Pete haunted Elise when she was watching *Jurassic Park II* on the couch in the basement with a boy she had a crush on. They were holding hands and if it weren't for the shadow they might have kissed. The boy thought she was weird and she cried after he went home that night because she hoped they might fall in love.

Pete haunted Jake when he played Halo late into the night with his friends. After hours of shooting and screaming at each other, they would quiet and the whole basement would feel like it was coming alive. Jake would see Pete at the edge of the room, near the tool area where the hot water heater clunked. He'd watch as Pete's barn cats walked along the pipes in the ceiling.

Pete haunted Hannah while she was playing house with her friends, Sarah and Mirabel. They'd be dressed up in Mom's gauzy outfits from the seventies, pushing baby carriages along the rust-red carpet, when suddenly his form shifted between the shafts of light from the high windows. Later he'd be waiting for her when she snuck downstairs to eat ice cream secretly out of the extra freezer. She'd get just a few spoonfuls into a pint before she felt his cold eyes on her back and would run up the stairs, skipping every other step.

Around the campfire all three of them said that they'd felt or seen Pete recently, not just in childhood. He's there when they come back for holidays, like the worn hardwood floor, the sagging sleeper sofas in the living room, like the white pines and hay field. Pete was part of the house. Recently when we all packed back into the old home for Elise's wedding, they'd felt him in the basement where all of her decorations were stored. I'd heard them joke about Pete when they'd been sent down to fetch vases or table cloths, but I didn't realize I'd made something that followed frightfully through their days. I'd manufactured the most terrifying story they could tell, their worst brush with fear. I wonder if he was gone would they still shiver when they stepped down the basement stairs? He had been so easy to create, I'd taken pleasure in the process, gathering his details (the cut glass, the road signs), but I hadn't the strength to kill him by telling the truth.

The big house is quiet. I lie awake, alone. This time a hoot from the loons, used as a check in with family members. It's a sharp sound, not haunting like their wail or tremolo. It sounds like someone yelling *hey!* across the water.

I list all the places I've heard loons. At summer camp. At that family camp. At boarding school in northern Michigan. Here again in Maine. I know them just enough to recognize their call and their red eyes, but they are still strangers to me.

In the morning my brother and his girlfriend are up early making breakfast. We have all been assigned meals to prepare over the weekend so that no one is overworked or burdened by our reunion. Their eyes are heavy with sleep and they shuffle around the tiles, bumping into each other like old friends. I watch them cook wordlessly and feel toward them an odd maternal loss.

My siblings don't need me anymore.

Maybe this is the curse of being the eldest. The first to all things, even uselessness. Over two summers I was tasked, unceremoniously, with tearing down the structures of our childhood. I took apart the swing set and lugged the metal parts to the dump. Then I demolished our tree house, half rotten and stretched by the growth of the two trees that supported it.

I make myself a cup of tea and sit at the table as they set up the buffet. We all sit around a huge table and eat a breakfast casserole. Rolls of steam from coffee and tea soften my family's faces. Jake's girlfriend offers me seconds. I let her fill my plate again even though I'm full because consumption is a form of affirmation, because yes is easier than no.

After breakfast, I walk up the driveway to a small rural graveyard across the street. Mom had asked to come with me, but I told
her no. I knew she wanted to talk about her cancer but I'm not
looking for death. I'm sick of talking about it and sick of reassur-
ing her that she'll be all right, which she will. After my divorce I
have needed to believe in good outcomes, not worst-case scenarios.
She wants to talk about what might happen if she's the two percent who don't survive treatment. This morning I don't want to
remind her of the other ninety-eight percent who would wake to
sunrise and lilacs, who would canoe, who would worry at the call
of loons in the night.

On the day of my wedding I asked the photographer to start her
round of picture-taking in the graveyard. I'd chosen the church
for its graves. They leaned so romantically, the stone soft from
the mouths of green lichen. I think I felt that somehow in lying
my way into marriage I was joining the host there of small town
people committed to life between a river and a hill, some of whom
were living, some of whom were long dead. Marriage was one step
closer to the grave in that it tied me down like a body that had
ceased to move. A corpse can go nowhere. It is bound to find its
beauty in the same rising and setting of the sun.

After showing the photographer out to the graveyard I swallowed a painkiller a friend had purchased for me off someone
who had a prescription. I hadn't had a drink in years and felt
entitled to relaxation on my wedding day, but the pill numbed
me so that I seemed to float, my body hovering over the church
boards, my heels skimming the grass. When I slipped into my
dress it was a cold as stone, and even though I'd just had it fit-
ted, it slid from my bony shoulders. I was wasting away. At the
altar I was so high I had to hold on tight to the prayer stool as I
knelt. I don't remember a single face in that crowd. Afterwards,

as we were getting our pictures taken, my gaze drifted over the churchyard to the graves where the afternoon sun was casting long shadows on the grass.

In the graveyard in Maine I find the headstone of a giant woman who traveled in a circus and, nearby, the huge, steel monument of a sea captain. One of the welds is coming loose and through its sides I can see the hexagonal combs of wasp nests. From a slight hill where the big family memorials spread, I can look over the big roof of our rented house and onto the flat lake water past the pines.

What does it mean that I told a lie that haunts my brother and sisters? Is the life of that lie important to them, their shared stories, their shared fear? If I come clean I fear we might all loose something.

Out on the lake my sisters and I drift in a canoe. The midday sun warms my shoulders. Hannah is in the bow powering the craft. I sit in the stern, steering. Elise is wedged between us serving as a weight and talking up the empty sky.

I say nothing about my lie.

We circle the shore, pointing out cottages that are well tended and others that are falling to rot. We watch kids cannonball into the water and wait patiently for a loon to pop up from the lily pads. The sounds of ripples, paddles, wind in the pines. The sound of human voices, and dogs and small two-stroke engines, music, cars. We canoe all the way to the far end of the lake where there are no houses, or docks. The sounds are distant, just ripple and pine remain. Looking back over the expanse of water where we came from seems very far away. Hannah and I raise up our paddles and let the canoe slowly spin in the shallow water. Our voices quiet to a whisper; we speak as if we might scare the loons.

My divorce.

Elise's marriage.

Hannah's plans after college.

Five years down the road.

Ten.

I ask Elise if she remembers skinny-dipping in Maine. Hannah would have been just a kid and deeply asleep that night. Elise smiles. Yes, she remembers.

It wasn't just my story.

We sit in silence as the boat spins. I feel their weight and my weight on the water.

Hannah looks up at the sky. *You've never seen Farmer Pete?* she asks me. I want to stay warm with them, heavy in that canoe, gently floating over lily pads.

Yes, I say. *I see him all the time.*

To My Siblings in a Time of Apocalypse

I. DEAR JAKE

WITH A JOB YOU GET a routine, that boring thing that you're probably afraid of getting. You wake up at a certain time, eat, get dressed, walk by the same people on the way to the subway, and sit somewhere all day with the same people. Since you don't have a job, since you're not out there having that routine, you won't notice that one day there aren't as many people, or that everyone looks sick and tired. There won't be office talk about this or that bug that's keeping everyone home and delaying meetings. You also don't watch the news or read a paper so you won't notice the headlines. You might read things online, or see posts on Reddit but for the most part, you drift above the normal world. You always have, as a little boy you were dreamy and soft, you slept late, your hair was like goose down. You have never been aware. We got our childhood dog because Dad was afraid you might be eaten by a coyote or a fox, you would have just sat there and watched the beast come to you. So I am writing to you first. It's a wake-up call.

Nick may have the magical ability, as the only born-and-bred Brooklyn resident in your apartment to read that there is something beyond the normal weirdness of the city at hand. His sensitivities will be alerted by something hungrier than usual in the eyes of the street musicians. He'll wake, in the night, like a hunter, to the sound of more sirens than he has heard on any other night of his life ringing through the buildings and bridge abutments like wolves howling in the forest. Listen to him, see his fear and know that you need to get out.

You can bring him and Kristin but not the rest of our roommates, there's just not enough space for them here. Leave the city before they figure it out. Load up Kristen's Porsche with only the essentials. You'll pack your musical equipment, even if I tell you that we won't have electricity for a while. I know its worth a lot to you and you probably can't imagine a future where you won't be able to plug it in to a wall. Maybe one day you'll gut the keyboard and find some important piece of hardware that'll save all of our lives.

The hard part for you will be leaving the city. Try to stay off the main roads. Follow Google Maps, if its working, and take exactly the route that you think no one else will take. Avoid waiting in traffic at all cost. Stay on the move, even if you drive in circles. Once you are out of the city, take the low roads back home. I've sent you an old-fashioned map, just in case. Remember, dirt is better than pavement. It'll take twice as long but don't worry; you'll get here. You'll know the way as soon as you are in the valley. I'll have dinner waiting for you and a bed made up. I worry about you more than Elise or Hannah, I don't know why that is. I always have. My little brother, you are such a sweet boy, I need to know you are safe, under the same roof, so that my dreams are no longer dark.

By the time you get this letter, you and Dave will be all moved into your nice house in the suburbs. All your wedding presents will be opened. Your honeymoon tan will have faded. You'll be lonely in your big house, out past the T. I know you'll notice it right away. You'll see it on the way to work; you'll read it a million times on your Facebook page and see it on the local news channel when you drink your coffee in the morning. You'll panic like you do about the flu and getting fat and you'll read all about it on WebMD forums. You'll text me, and I'll tell you to get out.

Getting Dave to leave will be the hardest part. I know he's planned for this, he'll want to stay and fight. He has a whole room where he stores his whiskey and his guns; he's prepared for this. You can bring your two fat cats; that's fine. There are plenty of rats in the chicken coop for two more cats to feed off of. But you can't tell anyone you are coming up here. I hate your friends, like deeply and truly hate them. I'm not saying that I want to see them die; I'm just saying that I want no part in saving them. All you need now is the family and Dave. He's a good guy to have around in this situation. He can't stay down there in the I-95 corridor, fighting off these things. Have you seen the eastern seaboard from space at night? It's like a wave of light, like a tsunami washing into the Atlantic coast.

Get off the interstate as soon as you can. Come up through the Berkshires and then along the river. You'll need to keep Dave calm because everyone hates drivers with Massachusetts plates. He can't speed or cut people off. You don't want to draw attention to yourself. Just follow the river; you suck at directions, so I'm giving Dave this map. I'll have dinner waiting for you when you arrive. You can have the big bed upstairs because I know you are afraid of dark windows on the ground floor at night. Everything will be okay. I promise I'll keep you safe.

3. DEAR HANNAH

I'm going to ask you to go against your nature. Right now it's going to sound awful, and I can already feel you getting pissed off like when I mock you for not using deodorant or gleaning kale. When you start to see people getting sick, don't help them. When the juice bar you work at starts offerings free clinics with an herbalist and cleansing pilates for those affected, you can't help out. You can't volunteer at the shelters, or hand out boxes of leftovers from the super high-end market to those with a hunger that even goat cheese and lemongrass can't fill. You, my beautiful sister who has always had hope, hope that the hungry will be fed, the dumb will learn, that our soap will no longer give us cancer, that our government will tell the truth, you are not wrong, but you will die if you stay and try to make things right.

We will start again. I promise you that we will live, finally, like we did those summers we worked together at the farm. We will wake with the sun and eat what we grow with our hands. Carrots from the soil, eggs from the hen house. The hens themselves we will stew in the fall and boil until they are soft and taste like a chicken was always supposed to taste. There will be no cancer-causing soap, we'll have to learn to make our own from the leftover lard from last year's pigs, and ashes, I think that's how you make soap. We'll have plenty of time to figure it out. Please bring CJ if you can. You two are perfect together in that wonderful love of youth where you look for in a partner the things that you most love in yourself. You two are like bookends to the same life.

I will comb your hair at night and put it in braids, so it doesn't tangle when you sleep. Believe me, this future is better than any other possibility. We have the chance to build something again. Everything that we hate, we can leave behind. We'll never have this opportunity again, ever, so don't do what your roommates are doing, don't stop to help along the way, think about yourself for once and don't feel bad about it. If any of us should survive, it should be you. You are kind and caring and without pride. You can tend to the garden. CJ can try to grow grapes and make wine in the basement.

Come down through Vermont, the interstates shouldn't be much of a problem, but it'll be safest if you follow the back roads home, you remember the way that we went last summer when we visited Mom's family farm in Cabot. Dinner will be ready when you get here. We'll spread mismatched linens over the picnic tables in the backyard, use all the nice dishes and light our meal with candles. We'll wake in a world in which we have all the chances to be good and true again.

Acknowledgments

I'd like to thank the insightful and inspiring writers who have shaped this book: Patrick Madden, Connie May Fowler, Ann Hood, Sue Silverman, Robert Vivian, Trinie Dalton, and reaching way back, Michael Delp, and Jack Driscoll who showed me what it was to be a writer. For those who donated to my campaign and funded my trip to the NonfictioNOW Conference in Iceland: your support helped me finalize these pieces and as promised, here is a book! Thank you to Rosemary James and The Faulkner Society, as well as Franz Wisner who believed in my essays and generously opened many doors for me at the Words and Music Festival. Thank you to my friends and fellow writers at Vermont College of Fine Arts, Goddard College and Interlochen Arts Academy, there are too many to name here. Finally and above all, I must thank my fiancé, Daniel, for fostering in me what I had forgotten to cherish, for giving me the time and space to write, and for inspiring me daily to live boldly. Words aren't enough, no matter how I craft them, to express what he means to me.